MACMILLAN MAS

GENERAL EDITOR: JAMES GIBSON

MACMILLAN MASTER GUIDES

GERARD MANLEY HOPKINS	*Selected Poems*	John Garrett
BEN JONSON	*Volpone*	Michael Stout
JOHN KEATS	*Selected Poems*	John Garrett
RUDYARD KIPLING	*Kim*	Leonée Ormond
PHILIP LARKIN	*The Whitsun Weddings* and *The Less Deceived*	Andrew Swarbrick
D. H. LAWRENCE	*Sons and Lovers*	R. P. Draper
HARPER LEE	*To Kill a Mockingbird*	Jean Armstrong
LAURIE LEE	*Cider with Rosie*	Brian Tarbitt
CHRISTOPHER MARLOWE	*Doctor Faustus*	David A. Male
THE METAPHYSICAL POETS	Joan van Emden	
THOMAS MIDDLETON and WILLIAM ROWLEY	*The Changeling*	Tony Bromham
ARTHUR MILLER	*The Crucible*	Leonard Smith
	Death of a Salesman	Peter Spalding
GEORGE ORWELL	*Animal Farm*	Jean Armstrong
WILLIAM SHAKESPEARE	*Richard II*	Charles Barber
	Othello	Tony Bromham
	Hamlet	Jean Brooks
	King Lear	Francis Casey
	Henry V	Peter Davison
	The Winter's Tale	Diana Devlin
	Twelfth Night	R. P. Draper
	Julius Caesar	David Elloway
	Macbeth	David Elloway
	The Merchant of Venice	A. M. Kinghorn
	Measure for Measure	Mark Lilly
	Henry IV Part I	Helen Morris
	Romeo and Juliet	Helen Morris
	A Midsummer Night's Dream	Kenneth Pickering
	The Tempest	Kenneth Pickering
	Coriolanus	Gordon Williams
	Antony and Cleopatra	Martin Wine
GEORGE BERNARD SHAW	*St Joan*	Leonée Ormond
RICHARD SHERIDAN	*The School for Scandal*	Paul Ranger
	The Rivals	Jeremy Rowe
ALFRED TENNYSON	*In Memoriam*	Richard Gill
EDWARD THOMAS	*Selected Poems*	Gerald Roberts
ANTHONY TROLLOPE	*Barchester Towers*	K. M. Newton
JOHN WEBSTER	*The White Devil* and *The Duchess of Malfi*	David A. Male
VIRGINIA WOOLF	*To the Lighthouse*	John Mepham
	Mrs Dalloway	Julian Pattison
WILLIAM WORDSWORTH	*The Prelude Books I and II*	Helen Wheeler

MACMILLAN MASTER GUIDES

MURDER IN THE CATHEDRAL

BY T. S. ELIOT

PAUL LAPWORTH

MACMILLAN
EDUCATION

First edition 1988

Published by
MACMILLAN EDUCATION LTD
Houndmills, Basingstoke, Hampshire RG21 2XS
and London
Companies and representatives
throughout the world

Printed in Hong Kong

British Library Cataloguing in Publication Data
Lapworth, Paul
Murder in the cathedral, by T. S. Eliot.—
(Macmillan master guides).
1. Eliot, T. S.—Thomas Stearns. Murder
in the cathedral
I. Title   II. Eliot, T. S.
822′.912   PS3509.L43M8
ISBN 0–333–37205–0 Pbk
ISBN 0–333–41725–9 Pbk export

CONTENTS

GENERAL EDITOR'S PREFACE

The aim of the Macmillan Master Guides is to help you to appreciate the book you are studying by providing information about it and by suggesting ways of reading and thinking about it which will lead to a fuller understanding. The section on the writer's life and background has been designed to illustrate those aspects of the writer's life which have influenced the work, and to place it in its personal and literary context. The summaries and critical commentary are of special importance in that each brief summary of the action is followed by an examination of the significant critical points. The space which might have been given to repetitive explanatory notes has been devoted to a detailed analysis of the kind of passage which might confront you in an examination. Literary criticism is concerned with both the broader aspects of the work being studied and with its detail. The ideas which meet us in reading a great work of literature, and their relevance to us today, are an essential part of our study, and our Guides look at the thought of their subject in some detail. But just as essential is the craft with which the writer has constructed his work of art, and this may be considered under several technical headings – characterisation, language, style and stagecraft, for example.

The authors of these Guides are all teachers and writers of wide experience, and they have chosen to write about books they admire and know well in the belief that they can communicate their admiration to you. But you yourself must read and know intimately the book you are studying. No one can do that for you. You should see this book as a lamp-post. Use it to shed light, not to lean against. If you know your text and know what it is saying about life, and how it says it, then you will enjoy it, and there is no better way of passing an examination in literature.

JAMES GIBSON

ACKNOWLEDGEMENTS

The author and publishers wish to thank the following who have kindly given permission for the use of copyright material: Faber and Faber Ltd for extracts from *Murder in the Cathedral* by T. S. Eliot; Penguin Books for an extract from *King Oedipus*, translated by E. F. Watling.

The edition used in this Master Guide is *Murder in the Cathedral* by T. S. Eliot, introduction by Nevill Coghill (Educational Edition), Faber & Faber, 1965.

Cover illustration: the painting of the murder of Beckett is reproduced by kind permission of the Cathedral Shop, Canterbury.

Every effort has been made to trace all the copyright-holders, but if any have been inadvertently overlooked the publishers will be pleased to make the necessary arrangement at the first opportunity.

SUMMARY

Murder in the Cathedral is T. S. Eliot's most successful play representing his triumphant development from poet into poet-dramatist, and although *The Family Reunion* and *The Cocktail Party* in particular amongst his plays are performed from time to time, *Murder in the Cathedral* remains the best and most enduring example of the poet's final creative phase. Alone of the plays produced in the verse drama movement which flowered in the years before and after the Second World War, *Murder in the Cathedral* has established itself in the contemporary theatre with frequent revivals on both the professional and amateur stages.

This Master Guide shows how the play grew out of Eliot's theory and practice and how its success gave fresh impetus to the search for a modern verse drama. Eliot considered *Murder in the Cathedral* a success as an occasional play but a failure as a model for a future verse drama. In content and style the play certainly matched its original occasion, the Canterbury Festival of 1935, and this Guide explains Eliot's approach to elucidating and reinterpreting martyrdom for a modern audience, but it also brings out the wider 'truths' the play has offered to readers and onlookers then and since; the play is shown to have 'meaning' beyond its central religious intention.

The meaning of the play is shown to be not merely the expression of ideas in the poetry but also the effect of the total impact of the play. The analysis provided here reveals the subtlety and care lavished upon action, structure, characterisation and verse, all contributing through dramatic form to the themes of the play. Where doubts have been expressed or weaknesses alleged by scholars and critics these have been considered both in the commentaries and in the account of the critical reception of the play.

Throughout this Guide special attention has been paid to the verse effects achieved by Eliot in *Murder in the Cathedral*, and the thematic links of the play to Eliot's poems of the same period are also demonstrated.

1 LIFE AND BACKGROUND

1.1 LIFE

T. S. Eliot (1888–1965) was the most influential poet of the twentieth century writing in English. He was an American, born in St. Louis, Missouri, of New England stock, but from the age of twenty-six he made his home in England. In England he played a greater part than any other poet in creating the Modern movement, a deliberate turning away from what was left of the influence of Romantic poetry and certainly providing a contrast to the last manifestation of that sensitive school of poetry, the Georgians. Eliot's changes of style were accompanied by a considerable output of critical works, forcing new views of old authors, and reinforcing his poetic revolution.

St. Louis, Boston and London gave Eliot the urban settings and imagery to be found in the early poetry. He created a waste land peopled by fugitives lacking assurance and certainty ('Preludes' and 'Rhapsody on a Windy Night', 'The Love Song of J. Alfred Prufrock' and 'Portrait of a Lady'), and he created poetry out of the spoken language of his day.

Eliot's own university education at Harvard, based on a package of courses in different disciplines (still typical of American undergraduate studies today), gave him his diverse academic background. The literary and cultural complexity of his earlier poetry reflected this background, and it was seen at its most effective in his great influential poem, 'The Waste Land'. Eliot's childhood at home in St. Louis on the Missouri river and on holiday in New England gave him two central images in his later poetry, the river and sea in *Four Quartets*.

Eliot rediscovered Christian belief after years of spiritual exploration without firm allegiance and turned to the Christianity of the Anglican church in the late 1920s. Henceforth all his work was overtly Christian, the main poems of this period being 'Ash Wednesday' and the *Ariel* poems ('Journey of the Magi', 'A Song for Simeon' and 'Marina'). His declared Christian allegiance signalled a deliberate turning to the theatre as the most useful method of getting his message across to a wide public. One senses that Thomas Becket was an 'Eliot man'. His story was a discovery of self, of the interweaving of his earthly nature and his relationship with God. The name of the martyr and its association with 'doubting Thomas' attracted the poet to a natural identification.

Two contrasted views of Eliot's acknowledgement of his Christian faith became evident in the 1930s. One group saw his declared religious adherence as a falling away from contemporary relevance; others saw the commitment as the source of renewed strength. In 1927 Eliot became a British subject, confirming fourteen years of assimilation. He was married twice, each time to an English wife, the first marriage being made extremely unhappy through his wife's mental problems, the second, after the death of his first wife, being very happy. Much of the more recent work on Eliot's life and writings has been concerned with the creative importance of the first marriage.

The success of *Murder in the Cathedral* led to a determined attempt by Eliot to establish a modern poetic drama, a campaign interrupted by the Second World War. Eliot completed the *Four Quartets* during the war, resuming the search for a viable poetic drama in *The Cocktail Party* and two further plays.

A useful diary of Eliot's life, relating events and works, is *T. S. Eliot: A Chronology of his Life and Work* by Caroline Behr, a Macmillan Reference Book.

1.2 ELIOT THE POETIC THEORIST

Early in his career Eliot wrote poetry with strong dramatic tendencies; later he wrote drama with strong poetic tendencies. Eliot's early poetry was characterised by 'dramatic' elements:

division into scenes, use of emotional situations, events and stories, characters reacting to each other, and the intonation and style of spoken language. Above all, in 'The Love Song of J. Alfred Prufrock', 'Portrait of a Lady', 'Gerontion', and 'The Waste Land' the poet's voice was masked by 'dramatic' voices which presented characters to us. These characters were limited people, negative in outlook, withdrawing from life. One of the characters of the 1919 *Poems*, Sweeney, was to become the focus of Eliot's earliest attempt at a drama, *Sweeney Agonistes*.

The struggle to escape from a single 'lyric' personality as a poet into the wider complexity and variety of masks and voices moved Eliot towards dramatic form. But the dramatic aspects of the early poetry should not be over-emphasised; as well as approximating to drama in its speech and personages it used a dense combination of descriptive passages and evocative symbols. The techniques did not necessarily signify that the poet would be successful in writing acceptable dramatic dialogue. Lines capable of being spoken by actors and lines which convey action as well as emotion and meaning are the true tests for a dramatist whether he writes prose or poetry.

This problem of spoken dialogue became the prime concern of Eliot's theory of poetic drama. Indeed, his qualification for developing a modern poetic drama was derived from his revival of a living verse for his poems, catching the intonation of contemporary life, using poetic forms associated with impersonation, dramatic monologues in the fashion of Browning, the use of dialogue, and his exploration of the theory of a poetic drama from his earliest creative years.

Eliot is important then not only for experimenting with a modern verse drama but also for prompting discussion of the problems of creating such plays in the twentieth century. His earlier critical theory reached conclusion in his *Selected Essays* first published in 1932, and Parts II and III of this collection were dominated by a discussion of dramatic form, particularly that of the Elizabethan and Jacobean playwrights. A second phase of critical theorising was completed by another collection, *On Poetry and Poets*, in 1957, just before the production of Eliot's last play, *The Elder Statesman* (1958).

Here are details of the key essays:
1. 'Rhetoric and Poetic Drama' 1919 (in *Selected Essays* 1932)

analysed dramatic speech in relation to situation, the character's view of himself, and our view of the characters.

2. 'The Possibility of a Poetic Drama' 1920 (from *The Sacred Wood* 1920) hinted at the possibility of a public for poetic drama despite contemporary problems. Eliot said there was a need to discover a new combination of dramatic elements.

3. 'A Dialogue on Dramatic Poetry' 1928 (in *Selected Essays* 1932) asked whether a poetic drama was possible in the poet's time.

4. 'Poetry and Drama' 1950 (*On Poetry and Poets* 1957). This discussed the extent of his achievement in *Murder in the Cathedral*, and in particular considered the need for a flexible verse capable of presenting both the mundane and the profound.

5. 'The Three Voices of Poetry' 1953 (*On Poetry and Poets* 1957) traced the range of poetic voices, from the poet speaking in his own 'voice', on to speaking through mouthpieces as in dramatic monologues, and finally to the full creation of characters in their own right.

In his poetry and criticism and later in his plays and criticism, precept and example for Eliot go hand in hand. In his theorising he asked, 'What great poetry is not dramatic?' The drama he created was an alternative both to earlier attempts at a modern verse drama and to the naturalistic prose of contemporary drama. T. S. Eliot is important as a dramatist because no other has persevered so long to construct both a theory and a series of poetic plays, and because he achieved a clearly successful place in the twentieth-century commercial theatre. He tried to give drama levels and dimensions comparable in language and structure to those of the novel, and he argued that naturalistic drama was too limited, particularly in its failure to explore spiritual experience. Theatre offered Eliot the opportunity to achieve a wider audience than the printed page offered. He believed his poetic drama would tap a deeper emotional experience and would effectively portray reality at more than one level.

1.3 PLACE IN ELIOT'S WRITING

The themes and approaches of Eliot's poems and plays are interlinked. The themes of the plays are found most explicitly in the poems of the 1930s, *Ash Wednesday*, the *Ariel* poems, and 'Burnt Norton'. The 'heroes' of the plays discover a greater reality by withdrawing from temporal concerns, but remain positive in their commitment to the spiritual. In all the plays Eliot stresses that both the saints and the ordinary folk are part of the one pattern. The central characters of the plays reveal an interweaving of the redeemed and unredeemed into the same interrelated experience. Some commentators have criticised the saintly example as too dismissive of everyday life, seeing Eliot as the poet of loss or deprivation (David Daiches, *The Present Age*), and indeed it is true that martyrdom, the loss of self in a higher purpose, characterises his work from 'Prufrock' to *The Elder Statesman*. In projecting this vision *Murder in the Cathedral* is certainly the most triumphant and unequivocal. The religious aspect of human experience was not concealed by the surface as in *The Cocktail Party*. Martyrdom and sacrifice of self is the subject-matter as well as the theme in *Murder in the Cathedral*.

Sweeney Agonistes, originally published in separate parts (1926–7), embarked on an oblique version of this theme of the character separated from those around him by a greater awareness of sensitivity, a theme which only disappeared with the writing of Eliot's last play, *The Elder Statesman*. *Sweeney Agonistes* was complete in its incompleteness. Written as 'Fragments' it looked to European Expressionism rather than English theatre (see section 7 on Modern Verse Drama), and was a forerunner of the Theatre of the Absurd and of the vaguely menacing Pinteresque world of the play without a plot. Neither it nor Eliot's next dramatic novelty, the pageant called *The Rock* for which he wrote the Choruses, solved the problems Eliot saw as besetting poetic drama in the twentieth century. But the pageant shared some of the solutions discovered in *Murder in the Cathedral*, written as it was by invitation for an occasion. What had been established in Eliot's poetry became part of the texture of his drama: the mixture of the elevated and the ordinary, the contrast of everyday banalities and divine intervention into human history. Many found *The Rock* more banal than elevated, but the Choruses with their interesting experiments in rhythm were still read long after the pageant was embarrassingly set aside.

The Rock was an essential step in Eliot's theatrical apprentice-ship. In it he taught himself how to write choral lines in Greek fashion and in the style of the English morality play *Everyman*. Eliot found he could combine the elevated mode of the Authorised Version with the mocking satirical tones of a contemporary voice, a formula matching majesty with mockery. A request for a pageant play to raise funds for Church building, then, started Eliot off on his quest for a modern poetic drama. The effectiveness of *The Rock* Choruses ensured that the device would become an important feature of *Murder in the Cathedral*, although in the latter the effects were more varied and dramatic.

1.4 THE OCCASION

The Canterbury Festival had begun in 1928 with John Masefield's *The Coming of Christ*. Canterbury was not only the arch-diocese of the country; it was the most ancient Christian shrine in the land, sanctified by the 'hooly blisful martir' whose cult was the reason for Chaucer's Canterbury Pilgrims' journey. Naturally, plays connected with the Saint featured in the Festival productions, Tennyson's *Becket*, for instance, and Binyon's *The Young King*. When George Bell, Bishop of Chicester, invited Eliot to write for the 1935 Canterbury Festival the poet still chose the martyr for his subject despite a 1932–3 production of Tennyson's play.

The conditions were congenial to Eliot. He had a Christian subject and a Christian audience to be gathered at one of Europe's most famous Christian shrines. He had a director with whom he could work, and he had the chance to further the cause of poetic drama. The topic of martyrdom attracted Eliot, as did the nature of the event and its significance for a modern audience. That significance was brought out through the Choruses, and the emotional structure of the play is based on them rather than on Thomas's exercise in self-analysis. For that was the point of the Festival; the ordinary human response to the exceptional event, the martyrdom which repeats and reminds us of Christ's own sacrifice. Ritually the play comments afresh on an act whose meaning may have been lost in the familiarity of the outward story.

In the week beginning 13 June 1935, in the Chapter House of Canterbury Cathedral, *Murder in the Cathedral* was produced as the ideal occasional play. The play was carefully written to order, with length, number of characters, theme and completion date all determined and accepted. The critic Herbert Howarth saw the play as being powerfully attractive to British audiences of the 1930s. The play was not far removed from much drama enjoyed by the nation-wide amateur theatre movement, and the central figure was a national and religious hero whose story was taught in every school. Another activity possibly contributing to the favourable reception accorded to the play was the widespread fashion for teaching elocution which created an audience who found choral speaking congenial and attractive.

Eliot himself continued to stress what he saw as the limitations of his considerable achievement, in 1959 calling the play 'a period piece and something quite out of the ordinary'. This view reflects Eliot's concern that the play was 'a dead end' in his attempt to create a modern poetic drama, but it should also be emphasised that having solved the personal predicament of his faith he was now ready to relate the situation to a wider public.

The modern poetic dramatist Christopher Fry noted that although Eliot's play was written for a specific audience it went on to attract much larger ones. It achieved great success in London, was transferred to a touring production in England, and proved an exciting revelation to the WPA Federal Theater in the USA. To Robert Speaight, one of the early Beckets, it meant there was an audience for poetic drama 'under certain conditions'. The launching of that new genre took place at the Mercury in Ladbroke Road, London, not a club but a small theatre seating only 136. A run there starting in November 1935 lasted for 225 performances before going on tour. A second phase of poetic drama was introduced when Ashley Dukes revived the Mercury in the years 1945 to 1948.

Productions of *Murder in the Cathedral* continue in both professional and amateur theatres, on tours and in repertory, and in what the critic Francis Fergusson has called 'the limbo of the academic theatres all over the world'. It has established itself as a twentieth-century classic, the principal survivor of the poetic drama it was intended to inaugurate. It has been recorded on LP and on film. The Old Vic company brought out the record in a production directed by Robert Helpman, commended for its clear projection of the story line. There is also an excellent Argo recording with Robert Donat as Becket. Eliot himself felt that the film version had made the meaning of the martyr's rôle clearer, and perhaps nearer to what might have been achieved had he written the play for a London theatre and not for the Canterbury Festival. The film was more episodic in its narrative treatment, and some criticism stressed its more realistic style.

1.5 THE PLAY'S TREATMENT OF HISTORY

The play had the advantage of referring to a well-known, highly dramatic story of a confrontation between two powerful personalities, both historically and spiritually significant. The story was taught to all as a central 'myth' of the English nation. Although Eliot chose not to focus his action upon the conflict of King and Chancellor, it broods over the play, putting pressure on Thomas and making the spiritual dilemma real by providing it with its context in this world; the struggle between Henry and Thomas is embedded in the fabric of Eliot's play despite its not being the action itself. The three expected temptations are all directly related to Henry: the good life enjoyed by those in favoured circles of power; alliance with the King by acting as Chancellor again; joining the faction against the King. Eliot does not deviate from tradition and history at all, but takes the narrative into another plane of existence entirely.

The historical tale becomes an example not just of something happening in time but of a sequence leading to a timeless moment. In the opening of the play the historical events are interwoven with emotional fears expressed by the Chorus, and their reactions dominate our response. Later it is the meeting of Becket and the Knights that comes from history while the agonies of the Chorus become ever more dramatically intrusive. The Sermon is based on hints from contemporary records about the address which Thomas actually gave, and it explores the central purpose of the play, the significance of a martyr in history. The use of an historical subject facilitated the invention of a modern verse play partly because an audience accepts heightened expression as natural to historical settings.

2 SUMMARIES

AND

CRITICAL COMMENTARY

PART ONE

First Chorus 'Here let us stand'

Summary
(1–50) The first Chorus starts the action, establishes the situation, and sets time, place and atmosphere. The women reveal expectancy at Thomas's return, but fear the unpredictable. This Chorus creates a sense of waiting, of an interlude, and of the passing of time. The apprehensive Chorus approach the Cathedral full of premonitions. A confusion between safety and threat fills their minds. They experience a compulsion to be present, to 'bear witness' to events beyond their control. From the opening questions the Chorus move into the second paragraph of natural images representing the seasonal cycle, but even this is disturbed by recollections of martyrs, by hints of Peter's denial of Christ. It draws a contrast between personal comfort and the discomfort of acknowledging allegiance to God. Thomas's return is associated with the disturbance of equilibrium, even a breakdown of the natural order.

Commentary
The Chorus are expository in the fashion of Greek drama. A story known in outline and in detail is hinted at. They are not removed from the action, and they register its impact upon the ordinary people of the time. The effect is also universalised by identifying the audience with the Chorus. We all 'bear witness'. We ask,

'What does it mean to us?' The Chorus establish an identity and a mood. (1–5) The verse underlines movement, a hesitant arrival. The lines are broken up into parcels of words suggesting insecurity and indecision. (9–12) Eliot creates melodic vocal effects through his use of vowel sounds, and these and the length of line are carefully modulated. (10–11) A long line with strongly emphasised consonants prepares us for the next line in contrast. There is a sudden change in the rhythmic effect, short words creating expectation and suspense. The key word is 'wait', and this is repeated eleven times in succeeding lines in expectation of a crucial entrance. (14) Eliot uses an effective short-hand image of Peter denying his Master, thereby indicating a relationship between the Chorus and Thomas without explicit statement. Who will deny his Master? Will it be Becket or will it be the people? There is to be temptation, but only the dramatist is aware at this point. (18–19) 'Seven years' precisely dates the occasion in 1170. Seasons, location and foreboding are now combined with exposition. (23) Here we have the first appearance of a reference to 'suffering' (see comment on line 208); the people have been subjected to external action. (30–5) The Chorus shun awareness and consciousness, and a fear of going forward breeds in them a state of immobility ('Fear in the Way' was Eliot's first idea for a title). (31) 'death from the sea' is an oblique reference to the historical fact of the murderers crossing the Channel to kill the Archbishop, showing how Eliot always signals his action well ahead. (31–9) A cycle of four seasons depicted in disastrous terms. Winter, Spring, Summer and Autumn are seen as a vicious circle, symbolic of the Wheel from which existence a Buddhist would seek release. (42–4) 'Destiny waits in the hand of God' affirms the limitations of earthly power compared with God. 'A shaft of sunlight' is one of Eliot's favourite images of moments of vision, an awareness outside time. (48) 'Shall the Son of Man be born again?' Nativity and martyrdom are one; the identification of Death and Birth if a favourite paradoxical theme in Eliot's poetry, particularly in 'The Waste Land' and 'The Journey of the Magi'. (49–50) 'There is no action'. At this point in the play they witness without consent; they do not wish anything to happen. Already we are pointed towards the focal subject of the play, namely, acceptance of the true meaning of martyrdom in turn by Thomas, Chorus and audience.

The Priests

Summary
(51–69) The Priests are the first individual characters in the play. The first is elderly, the second is younger, and the third is more thoughtfully aware than the other two. The three Priests also speak more wisely than they know at times, but when they are present we are brought close to historical reality and to Thomas as Archbishop. They are critical of temporal as opposed to religious concerns for power.

Commentary
(51–2) The First Priest picks up the words of the Chorus (lines 18–19) creating the impression that time passes. (53–8) The Second Priest reminds us of the internationally political aspect of the conflict. (59–65) The Third Priest describes the English context to the wrangling, and concludes meditatively that political manoeuvres solve nothing. By this stage Eliot has provided us, in the speeches of the three Priests, with the first three temptations later to beset Thomas: 'living and partly living' (in the Archbishop's case at a very pleasant level), choosing between King and Pope, and backing one or other of the factions in the country. (66–9) Just as the Chorus speak better than they know at times so the First Priest notes that men have forgotten their best ally, God. In his 'unredeemed' state he makes it sound like a clerical cliché instead of the central truth the play shows it to be.

Messenger

Summary
(70–110) The Messenger moves the action forward and performs the traditional part of his rôle in bringing the dimension of other scenes to the stage. This version also introduces humour as he describes Thomas's triumphant if anxious return, an event which occurs more comfortably off-stage. The Messenger has individuality, relishing his news. In the first version of the play he was called the Herald. He has two speeches, the first stating the facts, the second giving an interpretation. He takes delight in demolishing his earlier picture to leave the Priests glum and full of

foreboding. Thomas's quoted words prepare us for the expectation he has of his own death.

Commentary
(78) 'Two proud men' stresses not only the reasons for the personal and public struggle with the King but also Thomas's own individual spiritual problem. (85–96) Pomp and excitement are brought out, but we are also reminded of Christ's entry into Jerusalem and the sequel of his death. (92–3) 'Precious relic' is another signpost in the play forecasting what is going to happen. (97–110) His language, despite his promise (71), tends to be orotund if not circumlocutory. His style mirrors his personality, and like Polonius in *Hamlet* he is delighted with the effect he has on his listeners.

The Priests debate the return

Summary
(111–43) Again the Priests rehearse the temptations of worldly matters, and remind us of Thomas's central weakness, his pride. When mankind turns to God only then will self-seeking end. The Three Priests are carefully differentiated, and they explore varied aspects of the uncertainty.

Commentary
(111–24) The First Priest's language is dominated by abstractions expressing human obsession with temporal power. He still sees it all in past terms, but indicates the problem of Thomas's pride. (125–36) The Second Priest returns to the themes of the passing of seasons, of waiting, and of a leaderless Church. He manages a tentative optimism, as yet quite unsupported by any facts. It is enough that the Archbishop has returned. There is some consolation to be gained from the assumption of spiritual responsibility. (137–43) The Third Priest, the most aware of the trio, puts the situation into a philosophical or religious context. The Wheel of Fate (see commentary on line 216 'the wheel') image is used to convey a sense of inevitability; a new stage has come and they must undergo it. All three are troubled by the Church's involvement in power politics. (141–3) 'Until the grinders cease'. This

phrase, echoing Ecclesiastes xiii. 3–4, adds a prophetic tone to the passage and an awareness of impending doom.

Second Chorus   'Here is no continuing city'

Summary
(144–95) The Chorus express the purely human situation into which the returning Thomas has intruded. Their suffering lacks Thomas's knowledge so that their advice is exactly contrary to what he has decided, and they cannot bear the thought of real change, the familiar being preferable to the unknown consequences of the Archbishop's return.

Commentary
Short lines describe the ordinary daily round; longer flowing lines develop fear and foreboding. (144) The first line, expressive of uncertainty, ironically recalls Hebrews xiii. 14, which suggests the things of this life are unimportant, a wisdom not yet achieved by the Chorus. (145 and 150) Contrasted images are used to emphasise key points of interpretation: 'Uncertain the profit, certain the danger' and 'you come with rejoicing, but you come bringing death'. (146–51) The repeated 'late' and 'doom' create a mood of lamentation. These lines have the authentic ring of a Greek Chorus, such as the Chorus of Theban Elders in Sophocles's *King Oedipus* (Penguin, trans. Watling, 1947):

> With fear my heart is riven, fear of what shall be told.
> O Healer of Delos, hear!
> Fear is upon us. What wilt thou do?
> Things new, or old as the circling year?

(152–83) 'We do not wish anything to happen'. For the poet this speech describes life without God, 'living and partly living'. It exudes normality, the daily round, the yearly cycle, a natural order mixing success and disaster in a manner fully expected, and it mixes the apprehensions of ordinary folk with humour, 'some not able to'. (184–95) The short lines of everyday expectations break down, giving way to lengthening lines of increasing agitation, combining fear of Thomas's return and awareness of a fate not controlled by the usual realities. (192 and 194) Internal rhymes increase the air of obsessive concentration on simple nightmares, 'shades' and 'strain on the brain', with the repeated sonorous effect of 'doom' and the pathos of being 'small'. The two kinds of verse used in the Choruses have now been introduced: long, free-flowing lines and short, more regular lines.

Thomas's first appearance

Summary
(196–217) The Second Priest, already established as the optimist, the Archbishop's man, admonishes the Chorus and completes the build-up to Thomas's entrance. This priest's colloquial speech restores the naturalistic plane, and the humour brings us back to earth. His limited, practical mind, his affection and loyalty, all prepare us for the everyday world of Thomas's presence in England as the returned Archbishop of Canterbury. The priest's last lines are overheard by Thomas.

The style of Thomas's first speech provides a complete contrast. After the word 'Peace' Thomas does not address the waiting people. The word is a challenge: not an exchange of greetings, but a picking up of the Third Priest's awareness. It is an important word because it describes a central objective for all of those participating in the action. Some patiently suffer (Chorus); others mix action and patience by avoidance of the real challenge (Priests); some actively intrude (Knights); all three are trying to remove disorder and disturbance from their lives. Only at the centre is there the unchanging stillness of God; yet it is the initiating point of all action (the Wheel).

The Messenger has prepared us well for Thomas's entrance which is no surprise. His words, however, are surprising. The action of the play stops while Thomas voices one of the key statements in the play, anticipated in the Chorus and about to be developed in the Temptations. At the heart of the play lies this speech based on double meanings.

Commentary
Thomas's speech is non-naturalistic. His words become gnomic and full of balanced paradoxes, an oracular delivery appropriate to a profounder plane of spiritual mystery and of an awareness

beyond that of the other characters in the play. The passage is quite deliberately confusing and challenging so that it can return in a new form in the Temptations. The lines are spoken in Thomas's pride so that it is entirely appropriate for the Fourth Tempter to cast these sentiments back at him (591–9). It is the context of the statement that renders it true or false. It is thus central to the whole play's ambiguity and to Thomas's problem (667–8).

(208) 'Suffer'. Two meanings may be distinguished: (i) to experience anguish, something unpleasant and painful, torment; (ii) to undergo, to have something done to you, to permit or allow ('suffer the little children to come unto me'). Suffering is seen both as pain and as passive acceptance. Action is our doing something; suffering is having something done to us. From the two meanings we may define four complexities:

> (i)   experiencing pain or anguish
> (ii) undergoing something
> (iii) allowing something to happen (submission)
> (iv) consenting to a happening (participation).

The complexities grow out of the double meanings balanced against each other:

Act	Suffer
Agent	Patient

Thomas's words at this point span the developing experience of the Chorus. What happens to us is one thing; understanding and knowledge of what happens to us is another. We are aware of experiencing something, but we cannot explain its significance. This is a double suffering. The Chorus know (are aware) that they are suffering; they do not know (do not understand) the significance of what is happening to them. When they understand and consent, then action and suffering are one. (209–10) 'Suffering'. Mankind has free will with consent to act, to serve selfish needs or God's will. The desirable condition of 'suffering' is that of being subject to conditions initiated by God. (210–11) 'Patient'. In the lyric Section IV of 'East Coker', the image of the patient appears in an extended form. A patient is attended by a wounded surgeon and a dying nurse in a hospital 'endowed by the ruined millionaire'. The patient is (i) one undergoing treatment, an action beyond himself, and (ii) one enduring and suffering. (211–17) 'Pattern'.

There are two patterns discernible in the play: (i) the drama itself, the murder and its re-enactment in the play as ritual with audience participation, and (ii) the order of time (the Wheel) and temporal existence informed by God from 'the still point of the turning world' ('Burnt Norton') at its centre. (216) 'Wheel'. The Wheel is a recurring image in Eliot's poetry, particularly that of his middle years. The whirling movement of the Wheel at its periphery suggests maximum, frenetic activity and non-awareness. The connection with the still centre, God, is not realised. The whirling image was explored first in the play on words found in *Ash Wednesday, V*:

> Against the World the unstilled world still whirled
> About the centre of the silent Word.

The step-by-step transformation of the vocabulary symbolises the slow and difficult achievement of peace and understanding contrasted with the fretful, agonised activity of the surrounding world. Such knowledge is sought and gained, at times tentatively, only rarely in triumph. In Eliot's 'Coriolan' poem, 'Triumphal March', the knowledge of the still centre contrasts with the grandly ridiculous world of flags and trumpets, and it is hinted at again in 'Difficulties of a Statesman'.

In 'Burnt Norton' the image is central to the whole poem, and a version of the still centre is found in the epigraphs quoted from Heraclitus, a Greek philosopher in the fifth century BC who stressed the impermanence of living things. The first epigraph may be translated:

> Although the central intelligence is common to everybody, everyone lives as if he had his own separate wisdom and understanding.

This central theme of 'Burnt Norton' describes much of what *Murder in the Cathedral* is about. We are part of one single design common to us all; yet we as 'many' act as if we had only our individual concerns unconnected with God. The second epigraph, 'The way up is the way down', hints at the complexity and unity of opposites found in *Murder in the Cathedral*. Above all, in 'Burnt

Norton' II the point of resolution of opposites is offered as the
still point:

> at the still point, there the dance is
> But neither arrest nor movement.

An ordered pattern originates there at the centre.

In religious terms the major connection lies between *Murder in
the Cathedral* and 'Burnt Norton'. In terms of living in the 1930s
the connection with the 'Coriolan' fragments is more important
because the two pieces embody ways of life, public advancement,
political assertion, the pomp of power, negotiation and manipula-
tion rejected by Thomas in the play. The saint has other objectives, as explicitly stated in *Four Quartets*:

> But to apprehend
> The point of intersection of the timeless
> With time, is an occupation for the saint.

The Priests and Thomas discuss his return

Summary
(218–29) The down-to-earth Second Priest returns us to the
immediate present. There is a reminder of the time-scale through
the repetition of 'seven', taking us out of the timeless order
glimpsed in Thomas's words. The Second Priest admits they could
have been better prepared, but he means in respect of warming
rooms for occupation. (230–46) Thomas, assuming his Archbishop's rôle, for a moment also re-enters time, and gives details of
his enemies. (247–54) He tells us that the action of the play
depends on God's will, not on human choice.

Commentary
(232) There is a hint of a slight reproof. He appreciates their
kindness but he has weightier matters on hand. He has only a
temporary respite. (246) The First Priest's simple query, 'But do
they follow after?', has a hint of the shadows to come. (247) The
powerful image of commitment warns us that the moment comes

precipitately, not as a logical sequence of cause and effect. Everything depends upon God willing it. (251–4) Eliot is again pointing to the next stage of the action. Thomas refers to the figures about to enter as 'shadows', all of them, he believes, ghosts of the past. Confidence and pride are conveyed by the simplicity of his command, 'All things prepare the event. Watch.' He is not expecting any surprises. (253) We are given another dramatic hint. What he does now is important, even more so than his death which is to follow.

First Temptation

Summary
(255–322) The Temptations begin, and Thomas responds to the first three with cocksure mockery and implacable superiority. Temptation is at the heart of the play. The First Tempter offers enjoyment of the 'good life'.

Commentary
(255–75) Ease of living is suggested by the amusement in the lightness of the feminine rhymes. A 'good time' appears to be the refrain. (268–9) Eliot gives his lyrical moments in both poems and plays a wonderful wistfulness and nostalgia. Indulgence in earthly pleasures is obliquely but sensuously evoked with a classical air of contentment, as in Horace in the country or in a Virgilian bucolic. (272) The poet's sense of fun shows in the alliterative linking, the slightly overdone 'w' sound. (276–81) The 'new season' images have a contradictory force, snow on blossoms creating an illusion of age in youth. Thomas finds it easy to reject the commonplace yearning, and his response closes forcefully with a conclusive philosophical comment (276–81). (290) We have a third appearance of the 'Wheel' image, more forceful now, not merely indicating the passage of time. (303) To take life easy is the most usual temptation when the moment comes for action. (309–10) Venial sins, self-indulgence, the life of the flesh, do not involve major condemnation and would need but moderate penance. There is a hint here of the later stage of a graver sin, spiritual pride; Pride is one of the Seven Deadly Sins, a mortal sin. (319) Thomas admits that the impossible can still tempt.

Second Temptation

Summary
(327–94) The Second Tempter offers political power, using Church authority to achieve earthly ends.

Commentary
(323–7, 342) These typically balanced lines are reminiscent of Old English poetry, emphatic phrases linked by alliteration. (343–50) The rhymed couplets convey the neat rationality of the proposition, as well as having a sententious doggerel effect. (352–5) The Old English alliterative tradition is used in some Tempters' speeches. Thomas answers in kind. (355–9) An example of Eliot's adaptation of a style or an effect, in this case from Conan Doyle's 'The Musgrave Ritual'; lines which carry hints of secret rewards. (385–94) Thomas finds it easy to reject the Second Temptation. After all, he has wielded this power but chose to give it up. It is the last temptation from the past, and the next temptation will be concerned with future possibilities.

Third Temptation

Summary
(395–473) The devious Third Tempter argues for rebellion against royal power.

Commentary
His crabwise approach adds humanity to the abstraction as well as provoking Thomas's humorous riposte. By contrast the Third Tempter makes Thomas's superiority acceptable. Far from seeming aloof and priggish, Thomas in his shrewd awareness of a contriver is admirably human, and this sharpness is a characteristic typical of a Chancellor and politician as well as of a man concerned with his own spiritual welfare; Thomas's saintliness does not mean he is unworldy in his assessment of others. This confrontation does much for the humanity of Thomas's role, showing his ready wit, sharp perceptions and intellectual confidence. He is a man not easily overborne. (411–19) The Tempter's devious lines reveal a cautious and confusing approach to meaning despite the bluff,

ordinary, no-nonsense posture mocked by Thomas. The word 'Circumstance' figures prominently, and conflicting terms muddle the effect: 'enmity', 'alliance', 'enmity', 'friendship' and 'accord'. (460) In his various rejections Thomas seems to reserve his strongest contempt for factional politics and is dismissive of the Tempter's arguments for patriotic nationalism. (472) Thomas appropriately uses a biblical image of impotent former power.

Fourth Temptation

Summary
(474–599) The Fourth Tempter is not only a surprise in being there at all: his nature and his manner are different, confident and self-congratulatory (480), mysterious and mocking (482). The Fourth Tempter argues that Thomas should fulfil his innermost desires by seeking martyrdom to gain power over people beyond his death.

Commentary
The Third Tempter claimed to be a surprise but was not. The real surprise comes after the series of three with a fourth visitor different in kind. As with Becket, the audience's expectation was met by the completion of three, the fourth not being expected. (In Jungian theory, quaternities, or sets of four, consist of three of a kind, followed by a different, final element, like the three synoptic gospels followed by St John, or the Holy Trinity and the Virgin Mary.) (474–85) The first exchange establishes the different nature of this temptation. Thomas knows the Tempter because he comes from within; but being internal he has never been 'met' face to face. (485–500) The Fourth Tempter recites the three previous temptations, revealing an intimate awareness of Thomas's moral choices. The sequence leads logically to a final step (501), 'Fare forward to the end', itself a recollection of Thomas's own mocking challenge to the Third Tempter. (411) For the first time Thomas appears to have lost the initiative: 'What is your counsel?', a further example of the ways in which this Temptation is different. (527–40) The Fourth Tempter projects the vision forward for Thomas, his speech dominated by the command to 'Think'. (541) The closeness of Thomas and the Tempter is revealed in his little exchange. (542–60) The Tempter uses images of loss to reinforce

Thomas's fear that even his spiritual power is vulnerable to the effects of time. (547) Referring to 'the Wheel' the Tempter looks forward to his repetition (597) of Thomas's first speech in the play. A rhymed sequence once more creates a mocking tone which intensifies Thomas's desperation, the would-be martyr diminished to a man 'who played a certain part in history'. (561–2) Three questions reinforce our sense of Thomas's uncertainty, and in 574 he realises at last the nature of the last temptation, his innermost desires. (589–90) It is Thomas's own phrasing which triggers off the Tempter's repetition of Thomas's first speech. (591–9) The Tempter's use of Thomas's words reveals to the hero the danger he is in. One phrase is omitted: 'for the pattern is the action/And the suffering'. The Tempter urges that it is possible to sense the pattern, to see what may happen, and see that it does, and this urging seems to miss the true perfection of will-power exercised by achieving the centre, the unmoving hub of action. The emphasis in the Tempter's version seems to stress inevitability, 'fixed in an eternal action' and 'That the pattern may subsist'. The shift in emphasis is important because with Thomas's awareness on his lips the Tempter forces us to ask what we are to take as the meaning. Can we believe the event?

Dramatically and thematically the Tempter's quotation of Thomas's earlier statement is effective in bringing us up short but it has caused some puzzlement. The Tempter mocks Thomas with the idea that his Fate is out of his hands, and that surely it is proper to succumb to destiny when it is determined by God. If it is God's will, the suggestion goes, how can you do anything other than submit to martyrdom?

Thomas's response is delayed through the Chorus's intervention, but it does come and then it is reinforced by the Sermon: you do not seek what is presented to you for acceptance, but once it is there and inescapable the martyr responds unequivocally. Divine intervention comes spontaneously and suddenly; it is not contrived.

Chorus   'There is no rest in the house'

Summary
(600–64) Thomas remains silent for a few minutes. The Tempters have left individually, and the final temptation has been under-

stood but not yet conquered. Visions of Thomas's conflict are articulated by other groups, versions of his doubts attuned to their own points of view.

The Chorus are joined by the Priests and Tempters acting as minor choruses, and at one stage all three combine. They express disillusionment, confusion, doubts and dangers. The drama is about to produce its *peripeteia*, the turning-point when the action, after appearing to move in one direction, takes another. It builds towards a climax through the sneering chant of the Four Tempters, the alarm of the Priests, and the alternating fear and despair of the Chorus.

Commentary

(600–3) A menacing disorder in nature is brought out in long, flowing lines. The sibilants hiss agitation. The description suggests the darkness coming over the earth at Christ's crucifixion. (604–18) 'man's life is a cheat'. The Tempters mock man's ambitions and pretensions, stressing the worthlessness of the world's rewards. The detailed references give the play a contemporary mood. By the linking of general self-deception to Thomas's supposed 'illusion' the Archbishop is declared to be a particular example of a more universal malaise, and the data move from the particular to convoluted abstractions. (619) The Priests add to the agitation, using a seafaring metaphor, warning Thomas not to take risks amidst adverse elements. (625–35) All three join in chorus to express a sequence of omens presaging death, before the final Chorus of Part I. (636–64) The yearnings of apathy in the Chorus are still strong, and they still prefer a deprived life, bearable despite its unhappiness. The idea of a Godless world, however, is unbearable. Life may not have been Paradise, but what faces them is Hell, this state being represented in animal images. Evil seems to be winning, and mistakenly the Chorus beg Thomas to save himself, believing their future is bound up with his earthly fate. This stage is consequent upon Thomas's momentary lapse of faith, his temporary doubts, and his sinful pride. The Chorus know that evil is near, but do not know where true salvation lies. Thomas's preoccupation with self has removed the last assertion of goodness. (653) Both Chorus and Priests have to learn that safety will not be gained by escape, but for the time being the Chorus is overwhelmed by a powerful awareness of sin, 'a new terror has soiled us', without acknowledging its nature. The threat is conveyed in images of predatory animals and of mad creatures like the 'nodding ape'. Mad laughter is more frightening than growls; it mocks the normal laughter of the daily round, 'Living and partly living'. There *is* no escape from evil in the world or from death. They have to acknowledge the existence of wickedness in the pattern of life, to accept that man is not innocent. They must experience the horror of being separated from God, and must identify with the suffering world. The Chorus, for once, mirror Thomas's own doubts. He has still to sort out the difference between illusion and reality. The Fourth Tempter undermines Thomas's position and sanctity; the Chorus restores his awareness of their need and the part he must play.

The parallel to Christ's crucifixion is close here, the Chorus's fears reflecting the doubts of the disciples, but the 'triumph' of the Tempters and Thomas's silence are both temporary. (663–4) This is the moment of maximum weakness and indecision, a portrait of bewilderment without perception, 'save us, save yourself'. 'Save' has two meanings: (i) to save himself for the immediate present will mean his *not* saving them, and (ii) to accept his temporal destruction for the right reason will be to save himself and them.

Thomas's summary

Summary
(665–707) The proximity of Thomas's response suggests he has heard the words of the Chorus, but their conflicts are running parallel, he on his plane, they on theirs. We must assume that a version of the conflict has been going on silently within him, and he emerges from his silence to speak of his solution, which will be based on awareness of what God wills. The hitherto parallel paths of Archbishop and Chorus are converging, and Thomas's speech is an answer to their need. Compassion will replace ambition, and he will act appropriately. Sympathy instead of pride and arrogance will release him from the trap sprung by the Fourth Tempter. He does anticipate his fate, but he is assured it will come in God's time. He must not appoint himself as scapegoat.

Commentary
The turning-point of the play has been reached. The Fourth

Tempter has pointed out that Thomas's predicament is not different from that of the Chorus; he knows and does not know when to act and when to suffer. But Becket now shows a complete grasp of his situation; he will wait for the time to come for him to break out of his earthly self to serve God. (671–700) Thomas relinquishes the ambitions of the ordinary world to be one with God's purposes. Worldly yearnings would otherwise obstruct the way to spiritual perfection.

INTERLUDE: THE SERMON

Summary
Time has moved on a few days, from early December to Christmas morning 1170. The proximity of St Stephen's Day, the day of the first martyr, and the recollection of another Canterbury martyr, Archbishop Elphege, prepare the congregation for Thomas's own fate, and confirm he has now overcome the Fourth Temptation. The Sermon has two phases:

> (i) The first part deals with paradoxes. On Christ's birthday we mourn and rejoice. Peace has two aspects, the desire for a quiet life in this world, and the peace of identity with God.
> (ii) The second part describes the nature of martyrdom. Martyrdom demands human affirmation; martyrs are created as part of God's design.

Commentary
Eliot now demonstrates the central meaning of the play in a dramatically different style. In explanatory prose the significance of the whole play is summarised, the straightforwardness of the language contrasting with the earlier verse of Part I. Following the Sermon, Part II depends less on surprising turns of plot and more on theatrical effects such as the procession, the ritualised murder and the Knights' Apology, and on a variety of styles in verse and language.

The Text: Luke ii.14. The translation is taken from the Latin Vulgate version of the Bible, and this would be the one used by Thomas. It has a reference to 'Peace', and one of the more important themes of the Sermon. (5–6) 'passion and death' refers back to the opening Chorus of the play where Nativity and martyrdom are seen as one. (17–21) 'mourn and rejoice' reveals opposites combining in a single experience. Paradox is central to Eliot's mode of thinking. (22–41) 'Peace'. Thomas defines very carefully the difference between temporal and spiritual peace. (24–5) 'stricken with War'. This is the most contemporary reference to the 1930s. The scale of the First World War had made war fearful in a new way. (42–86) Thomas now relates Christ's Passion and Death to the repetition of that act by the martyrs who followed. (67) The Sermon confirms that the lesson of the Fourth Temptation has been learnt. The real martyr subordinates his will to that of God. (81–3) The playwright signposts the next phase of the drama.

PART TWO

First Chorus   'Does the bird sing in the South?'

Summary
(1–27) The second part of the play opens with a lyrical presentation of the passing of the seasons which builds up the dramatic tension of waiting. Symbols of fertility dominate this passage. The Chorus yearns for rebirth, and provides an effective link between the explanatory Sermon and the final upward climb to spiritual well-being. One year is ending, and a new one is about to start.

Commentary
(13–14) The Chorus picks up the words of the Sermon (40–1), 'not peace as the world gives'. (15) Another contemporary reminder of the years leading up to the Second World War. There is a growing understanding in the Chorus that renewal comes through God. (16) This line in particular stresses the preparation for renewal, for life out of death.

   The theme of death bringing renewal is now to be emphasised liturgically in the Introits on Saints and Martyrs. The juxtaposition of Chorus and Introits reinforces the same thematic point. The world is cleansed by death in winter, before rebirth in the spring, one of Eliot's strongest recurrent themes. (See 'Journey of the Magi', 'I had seen birth and death'.)

Introits

Summary

(28–62) An *Introit* is a sung opening prayer, particular to individual Masses, services celebrating the Eucharist, Holy Communion or Last Supper. Introits were sung as the priest approached the altar. (Introits are alternating 'versicles' or sentences with lines quoted from the Bible, particularly from the Psalms.) These Introits indicate the passage of time, the liturgical days between Christmas and 29 December, and they also continue the theme of saintliness and martyrdom. The first three feasts of the Christian year are presented; the fourth day as yet celebrates no saint. The words, the banners and the procession establish an air of excited sanctity even before the murder. The Priests' lines are a patchwork of quotations from the Bible.

Commentary

(29) 'Princes moreover did sit'. This Introit was in Eliot's mind at the beginning of 1935 in an article 'Notes on the Way', *Time and Tide*, No. 1, 5 January 1935, and he claimed that Becket no doubt would have preferred to be remembered with this Introit for Boxing Day in mind. It is also clear from this article that Eliot was thinking about the dangers posed to the Church from external interference. For Eliot the Church offered an acceptable home for the true sceptic, in contrast to the extremes of unthinking dedication represented by political forces of the twentieth century. Stephen was falsely accused by the temporal power. He forgave those who condemned him, a response clearly relevant to Thomas's own position. (41) Herod's murder of children under the age of two reminds everyone that we can all be involved in the operations of evil, not least the innocent. (53–62) The Priests focus on the day which as yet celebrates no saint's feast. (57–62) It is left to the Third Priest, as one might expect, to point to the possible conversion of an ordinary day into something extraordinary. He anticipates the intervention of brutal humanity, 'sordid particulars', into the pattern of history so that the 'eternal design may appear'. The lines emphasise the double aspects of happenings, the different interpretations that may be placed on events. An event in time is not ambiguous in itself, but everything may be subject to varied explanations.

The Knights arrive

Summary
(63–93) After the abstractions of the Priests the exchanges revert
to the dialogue of orthodox drama. The Knights arrive, bent on a
grim mischief. The Priests try to lessen the tensions and aggression
by offering hospitality. The Knights refuse the welcome. Thomas
speaks to his Priests, at first echoing their ominous expectations.
But he has put his temporal affairs in order. He has not willed his
fate, but has expected it and accepted it.

Commentary
(63–82) The short lines suggest the urgency of the Knights'
mission. There is a collective menace in the way they pick up key
words from each other – 'business' and 'King' – and the repetition
of 'Urgent' builds up tension. **(78–9)** The Priests' offers of 'Dinner
before business' and 'roast pork' are both grimly turned around
and mocked by the Knights. **(90)** 'business'. This word has already
been given a threatening undertone (75 and 78). Here and later
(117) it takes on further echoes, reflecting Thomas's awareness of
his destiny. Their 'business' may be something beyond their
comprehension. **(91–3)** More repetition produces an air of
menace – 'king', 'alone', 'matter'.

The Knights' accusation

Summary
(94–204) The Knights state their charge against Thomas, that he is
in revolt against the King. Thomas attempts to placate them, but
will not give way on the primacy of his religious calling.

Commentary
(94–103) The verse begins to rhyme as the Knights intensify their
anger in preparation for the act of murder. The repetition of the
accusatory 'you' helps to build a sickening crescendo of hatred.
Short words of contempt are used: 'tool', 'jack', and 'brat'.
(104–8) Thomas tries to defend himself as a loyal subject. At first
he offers only a minor proviso, 'Saving my order'. As they have
done before, the Knights pick up a key word 'Saving' (109–13) to
turn it against Thomas. **(114–16)** The Knights are unconscious of

the irony of their words, not least for the future significance of their act. (117–30) Thomas attempts to calm the Knights with measured responses. (121–2) 'The King! God bless him!' has the modern ring of a drunken, after-dinner toast and prepares us for the style of the Apology (starting at 423). (131) 'Now and here!' It is Thomas who pushes the situation towards a climax. Once again a phrase is turned for emphasis. The phrase has already appeared in a different form, 'now, and here' on the lips of the Third Priest (61). It has the effect of signalling the crucial importance of what is about to happen. (132–69) Thomas submits to the Knights' accusations. Good dramatic lines give actors their manner, move-ment and gesture. The drama lies partly in the language and partly in its rhythm and rhymes. The Knights use strong and implacable words like 'Absolve', and their attack is insistently reinforced by the clever use of half as well as full rhymes. The feminine rhymes have a snarling, contemptuous, lurching effect. (159–67) Thomas stresses, even exaggerates, his support for the King's temporal power, 'I would wish him three crowns', but he is resolute here and in following speeches about his own spiritual domain. (175) 'If'. History does not confirm that the King did issue definite commands. (176–93) This is the crux of the confrontation between King and Archbishop, between State and Church. Thomas em-phasises that God's Church must remain supreme in spiritual matters. The repetition of 'seven years' brings out Thomas's own remorse that he has allowed political conflict to deprive people of spiritual resources. (188–93) Thomas stresses his subordination to God. It is not *he*, Thomas, who puts the King in *his* place. While Thomas himself is not important, God is all-important. (194–204) The Knights' threat now becomes formal, preparing us for the ritual of the murder. Monosyllabic and fragmented lines reflect the impending violence.

Chorus of anticipation   'I have smelt them'

Summary
(205–44) In a succession of choruses Eliot evokes an experience of Hell, moving from the physical to the metaphysical or spiritual. Eliot had a talent for producing sensuous repulsion in his poetry, and the creature images here lack definition, implying a loss of all human identity in a frightening disorder without pattern; time

seems to have gone berserk. The lack of the human is finally traced to a lack of the divine. The awareness of God's design will come in the moment of understanding found by being, however briefly and temporarily, at the still point, in this case brought about by the death of a martyr.

The Chorus closely identify with a world labouring under some terrible, developing process. The world writhes, heaves, breathes, all dominated by a stench of death. The Chorus are forced to admit their knowledge of evil, and it pervades the kitchen as well as the corridors of power. Corruption is seen as a part of living. The Chorus have to acknowledge their guilt, their responsibility, their submission to a life which has no spiritual dimensions. It is a metaphysical Hell, the Void, where God is manifested as an Absence.

Commentary

The images present both a state of mind and a state of being. Eliot aimed at a horrific sensuality, creating a sense of evil in the minds of the audience. In a secular age Eliot felt that a physical presentation of a spiritual condition was necessary. The Knights stand for the secularist approach which sees the spiritual aspect as insanity or mistaken policy. Reptilian images represent formless forces, scavenging creatures suggest death, and even the beauty of flowers conveys mindlessness. The long, irresolute, wandering lines reflect aimless fears and loss of direction, with a focus on the subject 'I'. Not all readers have found this Chorus satisfactory, feeling that the passage is too extensive and overdone, even comically solemn.

(217) The 'I' in focus represents an admission; this is a turning-point where the Chorus identify with the situation only observed previously. The disordered world has moved closer to them, and now they recognise that they are part of it. (222) The change of direction is indicated by a question: 'Have I not known?' (223–32) The lines shorten into crisp definition, the sense linked by repetition of 'in', 'as well as', and 'woven'. (226) A resentful, critical tone is emphasised by the alliterative phrasing of 'plotting of potentates'. (233–43) The Chorus affirm their 'consent', that they are guilty of evil. Powerful verbs dominate the language, firstly revealing disintegration, 'torn away' and 'violated', and secondly submission, 'subdued', 'united', 'mastered' and 'domina-

ted', and the verbs are made more emphatic by their positioning in the lines. (236) This time 'suffering' is acknowledged to be consent. (243) A quotation from Shakespeare's Sonnet 129, changing the imagery of sin from animal to sexual. For a moment the Chorus are disgusted with their physical lives and are prepared for their vision of the greater spiritual reality. Once they are emptied of all desire they are ready for their timeless moment. Surrender to the spiritual must be absolute. (See the description of this in their final chant, 640.)

Thomas accepts

Summary
(245–303) Thomas has recognised the torment of the Women presented in the preceding Chorus. They will forget the moment in time and return to illusions, and only remember that moment of truth as if it were a dream. The Priests still do not understand what must happen. The Priests and Thomas alternate in dialogue which interweaves agitation and acceptance. Thomas now interprets for us what is about to happen. He has accepted God's pattern, and so the murder will be an act of necessity, a ritual. Destiny is awaited, and no demands or pressure need be put on God. Awareness of the danger of sin removes the potential for commission. Pure in motive, Thomas can await his fate with confidence; pure in purpose, he can influence the lives of ordinary people, here represented in the Women of Canterbury.

Commentary
(245) 'Peace, and be at peace'. Thomas repeats his first word of the play. Humankind, despite its readiness to take the easy way out, 'Living and partly living', has a contrary necessity to feel at one with the source of creation, with life, with vitality, with God. (257) 'Human kind cannot bear much reality, is a view echoed in 'Burnt Norton' I, 42–3. Full human potential cannot be fulfilled in the physical dimension. Life at a public and physical level is an attractive but transitory state. (262) The saint 'making perfect his will' is a central theme in Eliot's plays, *The Cocktail Party* and *The Confidential Clerk*, as well as this one, although in the later plays there is a more balanced attention paid both to the saints and those who lack the gift of sainthood. The saint's vocation is to make his

own will coincide with God's purpose. As the Sermon stressed, a martyrdom reminds us of Christ's sacrifice, and that is what Thomas's death achieves. (271–5) 'A wink of heaven'. Thomas is aware that God has entered time and he is therefore prepared for martyrdom. The saint does not evade his promised death; he welcomes it. Thomas's calm is contrasted with the furious and fearful agitation of the Priests still trying to protect him, and with the agony of the Chorus. (278–9) The *Dies Irae* is the most powerful of medieval hymns, 'The Day of Wrath' being the first words describing the 'Last Judgement', when all will be called to a divine account. (279–87) Short lines, chanted compulsively, convey a moment of static sensitivity, the terror of being lost to God, of losing the possibility of grace. (292–303) This is the lowest point of the Chorus's despair prior to their glimpse of a higher reality.

Thomas's death

Summary
(310–96) The Priests still seek to protect Thomas; he, just as positively, refuses to hide. The Knights assert their demands while Thomas says he is ready to die. There are mutual exchanges alleging treason. Thomas's last assertion of a temporal authority puts the Knights in their place as temporal and spiritual inferiors. It is one of the few moments in the play when we meet the man of history, forceful and authoritative.

Commentary
The murder is a beautifully contrived piece of stage-craft. It is de-sensationalised, an act of violence in ritual form and is led up to with a sense of inevitability which is as important to Eliot's theme of 'the time must be right' as it is to his achievement of theatrical impact. In the dangerous excitability and aggression of the Knights, the panic of the Priests, and the ultimate accompaniment of the *Dies Irae* off-stage, the passage moves with an implacable fascination and high emotionalism.

(310–15) Broken, short lines express the fear and anxiety of the Priests as they still try to protect their Archbishop. (316–22) Thomas is not passive in the face of destiny. (331–51) His command to allow the murderers free access looks backward and forward: 'You think me reckless' (332) and 'It is not in time that my death shall be known' (349). (347–52) Repeating Christ's sacrifice the martyr joins the people of the suffering world, suffers on their behalf, and heals them. (353–64) The Knights hammer out the doggerel rhythms of 'The Daniel Jazz', the poem by Vachel Lindsay which imitates a revivalist hymn. (366–75) Thomas's own references are dominated by 'blood'. He emphasises that his death is less a political murder than a Christian act. (376–9) The Knights make their unacceptable demands with the operative verbs strongly placed at the head of each line.

Chorus's expiation   'Clean the air! clean the sky!'

Summary
(397–422) The emotions of the Chorus are intensified while the murder is committed, but the lowest point is already past. All the pent-up emotion is released following the steady build-up to Thomas's death. Intense shame and mortification strike the Chorus at Thomas's dying, and they seek repentance, and this yearning takes them beyond everyday existence to an all-embracing awareness of their need for grace.

Commentary
(400–4) Even at this moment on the way up to spiritual knowledge the Chorus do not see it *is* the way. (403) Blood purifies here; it does not defile. The rain is a symbol of redemption. (417) 'This is out of time'. This is the moment of realisation, the wider dimension of human destiny but rarely experienced. History is suspended at this moment. The timeless has entered time, and consciousness dawns on the Chorus.

The Knights' apology

Summary
(423–580) In powerful contrast the Knights' flat colloquial prose emphasises the newly inspired spiritual state of the Chorus. Their self-justifications are clearly sophistries, and despite their plausibility they seem fraudulent compared with the assurance of the Chorus. We are meant to see through them, yet they draw some strength from appealing to presuppositions held by at least some of

every audience. The Second Knight's argument for the supremacy of the national state over any faith or religion, however universal its claim, has wide acceptance. The Knights live in the world of politics and state interference, of machinations and struggles for power. They are still in the world of time; the Chorus has had an illumination beyond time. Cocksure insolence is contrasted with faith and humility.

The Knights' names are those of the historical murderers of Thomas.

REGINALD FITZURSE The First Knight calls for a fair hearing, and begs the audience to listen to both sides and judge for themselves.

BARON WILLIAM DE TRACI The Third Knight justifies the act through a sense of duty. Four plain, patriotic Englishmen doing what had to be done. They echo the traditional cry 'King Henry – God Bless him!' De Traci argues that they were entirely disinterested and stood to gain nothing.

SIR HUGH DE MORVILLE The Second Knight claims he sought 'social justice'. The Archbishop was not an underdog. He tried to subordinate Church to State and then the opposite.

RICHARD BRITO The Fourth Knight argues that Becket chose martyrdom quite deliberately and therefore committed suicide.

Commentary

The disarming speeches of the Knights are a trick learnt from G. B. Shaw's play *Saint Joan*. In the same fashion the device underlines the contemporary relevance for the audience. The realistic parody of a politician's pleading turns to menace by the end, and intensifies the comment on the argument of political necessity under pressure.

In making their excuses the Knights lower the tension of the drama. Comic relief is introduced as well as another level of interpretation of Thomas's sacrifice. All they can offer is a superficial, worldly lack of understanding. The Knights' flat tones replace the choral, incantatory and liturgical rhythms. At best, their political platform oratory and after-dinner speech-making manage a hearty, vigorous *bonhomie*. The pseudo-intellectual analysis makes one think of debate, Parliament, mock-hustings, or the law-courts. It is a play within a play, a different world, a different language, a different mentality; again it all makes a thematic point for the poet. (547) Another genre is suggested by Richard Brito's 'court scene' technique which reminds us of the stock thriller or murder mystery tradition. He asks 'Who killed the Archbishop?' The surprise answer also has the ingenuity of a murder solution, but the idea that Thomas was 'responsible' for his own death is both a nonsense and a truth.

The Priests' final interpretation

Summary
(581–617) Unlike the Knights, the Priests have been changed by Thomas's death, and they see the Church as strengthened by his sacrifice. The Third Priest puts forward this positive view; the First and Second Priests express regret.

Commentary
They speak of the future in terms of discipleship in a world where mankind soon forgets. Fantasies and fictions help them forget. The reality of events is too painful; the 'hell of make-believe' is preferable to them.

Final Chorus

Summary
(618–50) 'Te Deum'. The Chorus concludes the play with willing affirmation. God's creation and their hope of redemption are accorded an ecstatic celebration.

Commentary
The preceding public statements of the Knights increase by contrast the sincerity of this coda of praise. Here the message of the preceding story is registered. The significance of Thomas's sacrifice has been revealed to them; they accept that they participate in the world which has connived at his murder. Martyrdom has been made meaningful to them as ordinary folk. They have renewed their relationship with God. Identification and consent replace apathy. Sympathy with the natural and therefore the divine order ends the play.

Some critics have argued that it would have been more dramatic if the Chorus had dispersed as the Knights ordered, and that the final paean of praise was less effective. But the affirmation of the martyrdom's significance on the lips of the Chorus is absolutely necessary for Eliot's purpose. Humankind has accepted the reality of God in the world, and for the time being the Church is renewed by the acknowledgement of sin and our participation in it.

3 WHAT THE PLAY IS ABOUT

3.1 A PROCESS OF AWARENESS

In the play we are faced with an heroic denial of the primacy of this material world, a stance which culminates in a violent murder. Different views of this central event are portrayed in contrast. Thomas's own interpretation of his death is that it serves God's purpose. The Knights grapple with their own non-comprehension, and argue that the death is suicide, the failure to seize the opportunities life offers. It is significant that when the time comes to react to the murder the Chorus speak the language of the *Te Deum*; the Knights speak in terms of the latest thriller (II.547), a form reflected in the ironic title of the play. The Chorus have moved from tentative weakness and failure to a consciousness of power and a far greater reality.

At first Becket, himself under temptation, is subject to the Wheel (see the Commentary on I.196–217), only vaguely aware as yet of perfection at the still point and of its possibilities. When he is face to face with his own pride he realises the limitations imposed on him still by his human nature:

> The last temptation is the greatest treason:
> To do the right deed for the wrong reason.
> The natural vigour in the venial sin
> Is the way in which our lives begin. (I. 667–70)

The play demonstrates how difficult it is for us still in the world to be aware of this different order of being. The martyr loses his will in that of God (Interlude, 65). Beyond human limitations Thomas has glimpsed divine perfection. At the conclusion of the play there are three levels of awareness apparent: Thomas who sees deeply into his relationship with God and has an understanding of the significance of his martyrdom; the Chorus who assent to Thomas's sacrifice and are emotionally aware of what has happened; the Knights who represent everyday interpretations of life, lacking a spiritual dimension of their understanding.

3.2 MEDIEVAL MARTYR AND THE NATURE OF MARTYRDOM

The clash between Henry II and his former Chancellor, Archbishop Thomas Becket, provides an historical framework for the drama. Other dramatists have exploited this story, which has the exciting elements of a broken friendship and the irreconcilable demands of Church and State. In his play Eliot largely ignores the potential force of this worldly action, and uses it primarily to provide a context for a study of martyrdom. The study concerns Thomas Becket's struggle to achieve Christian humility without falling victim to pride. The focus is not what happened in history but what meaning the event has for Thomas, for the Women of Canterbury, and for us. Thomas has to overcome the desire for personal self-assertion in order to subject himself to the will of God. He sets aside increasingly complex temptations until confronted by the most insidious one, the attraction of triumphant self-gratification which assured to a martyr 'a vision of eternal grandeur'. Becket stays as Archbishop of Canterbury to fulfil the demands of his rôle in life, but martyrdom comes as a result of acquiescence in what he sees as God's plan, and he has to purify his motives before he is fit for that martyrdom. Fear and courage do not enter into Thomas's reckoning, for these are the emotions of everyday life. The martyr's doom is foreseen by himself, and he forges that destiny, but he acts only when he is convinced that the sequence of events is divinely inspired.

Although causes and confrontations may characterise the situation in which martyrdom occurs, the martyr is not sacrificed to a cause. Steadfast to his belief in a higher order of being, the martyr repeats the scapegoat death of Christ, thereby bearing witness afresh. A few months before the play was first produced Eliot quoted 'The Ascent of Mount Carmel' by the medieval mystic Saint John of the Cross: 'to follow Christ is to deny self'. American critic Francis Fergusson attacked this aspect of Eliot's theme, the theological viewpoint that sees nothing of a human scale in our love for the Divine, that sees no link between Eros (human love) and *Agape* (the love of God for us). The things Thomas loved in his youth, as portrayed in the First Temptation, are not seen as evidence of God's bounty but as obstructions to a higher understanding. At its most extreme this view might be seen as suggesting that we are in Hell while we live according to this world's ways, and that only the saint's total rejection will reveal the path to Heaven. But Eliot always argued that his plays were aimed not at stressing the isolation of the saint but at exploring the significance of the saint for the rest of us. The existence of the saint does not invalidate the lives and aspirations of ordinary folk. The play does not argue that we must all be saints; it does argue that a view of destiny and history must encompass unhappiness, deprivation, misery, death and loss in the mass of suffering humanity as well as its pleasures, happiness and triumphs.

Eliot's Christian viewpoint is that the world is incomplete without God. The martyr re-enacts Christ's atonement for a world which lacks God. The martyr refuses to compromise and renounces the demands of this world, while the world in its turn cannot tolerate one who does not conform. The sacrificed martyr does not only witness to his own age. Indeed, the symbolism of the Wheel with its 'still point' indicates that Thomas's sacrifice is 'out of time'. For Eliot the moving wheel symbolises living in time, while at its centre movement disappears into the 'still' centre which symbolises God. The two images combine to represent the divine intersecting with the human, the point where God enters history. Thomas identifies with the 'still' centre:

> I give my life
> To the Law of God above the Law of Man, (II. 343–4)

The subjective self must become an object within the will of God; submission to that other dimension releases the potential saint from his human self and its motivation by this world and its ways:

It is not in time that my death shall be known;
It is out of time that my decision is taken. (II. 339–40)

The saint does not achieve his triumph for himself; he provides an opportunity for people to look at themselves anew. Chorus and audience are reluctant, but they witness and they accept.

To link the medieval story to its modern witnesses Eliot imposed a contemporary surface upon his twelfth-century content. The references mix medieval and modern experience: the Catherine Wheel, the pantomime cat, prizes at a children's party, tilt-yard skill, mill-stream, watchman, and the strategy of chess. Heaven and Hell were real to the medieval mind; Eliot's vision of fragmented horrors (II. 397) creates a modern equivalent for the twentieth century.

3.3   RELEVANCE OF THE HERO FOR THE 1930s

The conflict of Church and State has a significance beyond its medieval setting. The demands upon an individual's allegiance, for men of both important and lowly positions, have as powerful an impact on the modern age as in any past period. In addition to exploring matters of conscience the play examines the extent to which Church should meddle in matters of State, and vice versa, and these elements gave it added popularity in the thirties and forties although there is no identifiably propagandist angle.

Thomas's story of the individual's confrontation of the State as a matter of conscience provided a powerful allegory for Europe in the thirties when Hitler's Nazi Germany was in the ascendant. Hitler had come to power in 1933, and the position of committed Christians under an evil regime was highlighted by Eliot for all to consider. Audiences at the early touring production found a bold hero standing up to political authority and tyranny. Freedom of belief was the challenge demonstrated by Thomas, and for this element the play was highly regarded in the years prior to and during the Second World War. How far should the Church and its people accept secular evil when it is embodied in the State itself? It is as true now as it was then that the moral compromises a government may demand from its citizens may lead to acquiescence in evil. 1935 was a fearful year, and the anxious mood of the decade was perfectly caught by Eliot in the play. Appeasement of the dictators was offered as one response to the worsening situation, and was implemented as a policy. A world wearied by the huge sacrifices of the 1914–18 War did not want to face a renewal of Armageddon, and this shrinking from unpalatable realities is powerfully conveyed in the opening Chorus. The play closes with an affirmation of responsibility, an awareness and a declaration that one cannot opt out. The Chorus are contrite over the earlier refusal to halt the drift of 'living and partly living'.

In the play's confrontation between two attitudes, the demands of the flesh and those of the spirit, there was a moral challenge beyond religious allegiance. The aspect of inner integrity fascinated contemporary audiences, not least the command to do the right thing for the right reason. Further, people were interested in problems of destiny and free will. To what extent was individual man free to make choices in an age of universal conflagration and oppressive political regimes? The world was growing more insecure, threatening and terrible, and the Chorus spoke for ordinary people caught up in dangerous predicaments not of their own making.

3.4 MARTYRDOM'S MODERN SIGNIFICANCE

The nature of martyrdom is remote even from the experience of the committed Christian, but the mingling of strength and weakness in an individual is of universal interest, and in his greatness a martyr forces decision upon himself and upon others. The whole tenor of Thomas's struggle is to move its significance away from the personal and the particular to the impersonal and the general, from a potential saint obsessed with his own sanctity to the acknowledgement of being the agent of destiny. Thomas's inner struggle may be the least popular aspect of the theme, but the play tells us not to judge the act of martyrdom by external appearances but by internal integrity. Thomas's external behaviour puzzles witnesses within the play, and his motivation is bewildering or even mad according to the man-in-the-street logic of the Knights. But doing 'the right deed for the wrong reason' is hardly an extraordinary or exceptional experience, and this gives the play a

wider meaning for the non-believer, countering the proposition
that you have to be a Christian to enjoy this Christian play.

Nevertheless one of Eliot's major objectives was the dramatisation of the place of religion in modern lives. While the popularity
of the play may be traced partly to the relevance of the Man
against State confrontation and to the problems of the individual
conscience, the religious nature of the central experience is
unmistakable. An awareness of good and evil pervades the play.
The agony of the Chorus is derived from a sense of growing evil
and from a need to purge this taint from their being; a sense of
impending damnation forces them to a decision. Despite the
location of the original production in a cathedral, Eliot could not
depend upon there being an accepted body of Christian beliefs in
his audience, and his use of Christian concepts and symbols is
restrained, so that there is no fervour or fanaticism in the play but
rather an earnest assertion. For believer and non-believer alike the
strength of the play lies in its awareness of doubts, of backsliding,
of loss of perception and purpose, and of lack of commitment.

A particular religious or political view does not necessarily make
a piece of literature good and, above all, in a play it is the dramatic
form which recommends it to audiences. Structurally the play is
dominated by Thomas's determination to achieve God's purpose
whatever the cost and by the Chorus's terrified anticipation of
changed circumstances. The dramatic link between the two is
death; Thomas welcomes it while the Chorus fear it. The relationship of Thomas and the Chorus is the key element in the play.
Thomas restores to their lives meaning which they had lost, and
through his death they replace their awareness of hell on earth
with a final sense of fulfilment. His significance is thrust into their
world, repeating Christ's sacrifice to remind them that God has
entered history.

3.5 GOD ENTERS TIME

The significance of the one set apart, martyr or saint, in the lives of
ordinary people is central to Eliot's plays both before and after the
Second World War. In religious terms Eliot's plays purport to
show that a synthesis of the worldly and the spiritual can be
achieved and affirmed. Shared with *Four Quartets* is the concept

that we can all experience moments out of time, 'a tremor of bliss, a wink of heaven, a whisper'. In such moments we become aware of our spiritual natures, and the hero demonstrates this awareness to a doubting audience. In this play Eliot charts the acceptance of a religious conception of life, the reluctant admission of its place in lives less committed than that of the hero. The presentation of man's concern for his soul would have been less remarkable in earlier centuries, and to many readers or onlookers its survival into the twentieth century may seem curious or even irrelevant.

Each of Eliot's plays combines non-spiritual complacency with spiritual quest. The central conflict in each play dramatises the uneasy relationship between the two dimensions of reality. It is too much to expect the secularised onlooker to enjoy a play which leads him to believe he is missing something, and the presentation of the saint's solution as the higher way has annoyed those critics who see a spiritual interpretation of life as meaningless. Eliot had expressed the view in 1935 that contemporary literature was corrupted by Secularism, a state of mind in which awareness of 'the primacy of the supernatural over the natural life' was impossible. Eliot sought a literature 'unconsciously Christian', working through forms acceptable to modern taste; the abstract path is signposted with concrete evidence. The drama is nothing less than the rediscovery of a Christian myth which Eliot thought had been mistakenly rewritten in historical, political and non-Christian terms. After *Murder in the Cathedral* the role of the saint remains a central element in his plays, but it is reduced in overt importance. The prime aim of Eliot's drama is the destruction of illusion. In each play the hero starts off with an imperfect understanding of his sin or weakness. He becomes aware of what besets him and then does something about it. He is then able to face his destiny openly and truthfully.

4 TECHNICAL FEATURES

4.1 PLOT AND STRUCTURE

(a) Exposition and story

The play describes the final phase of Thomas's life. His past, his relationship with the King, and the conflict between Church and State are largely sketched into the contributions from the Tempters, although the tense opening Choruses do stress the struggle between Archbishop and King. The hint of crisis comes very early, and despite criticisms of the play which stress a ritual and static impression, it solves problems of narrative exposition and developing action very economically, while the theme is given extensive treatment. For his exposition Eliot was able to assume that most people who went to see the play knew the story in its basic essentials.

The story is simple enough. The Archbishop returns from France to lead his Church, determined to face the possibility of conflict with the King, despite advice to the contrary from his attendant Priests and despite the evident fears of the ordinary Women of Canterbury. He preaches a Christmas Day sermon on martyrdom, and after further vain attempts by his Priests to prevent his death he is killed by four drunken Knights.

Instead of widening the narrative span the dramatist chose to concern his action with a very narrow point of decision, an interior action with a very powerful impact. The story embodies the theme without moralising: Parts I and II are not didactic, and the Sermon is only partly so. Eliot relied on minimal stage directions, and the whole presentation has a universality beyond its historical setting.

(b) Formal structure

The play's dramatic effect is quite different from that of situation plays, and its form is important in organising the response of the audience; a simple line of action without digression, parallel plot or sub-plot is graced with the ceremonial grandeur of a ritual. The pattern of the play is one of development, contrast and balance, and like a church service the various phases contain the true action of the play. Like the Eucharist, Communion or Mass the play provides a symbolic pattern of dynamic emotional changes. A process of purgation leads to a state in which Thomas may 'make perfect his will' and the Chorus may identify with the event.

The parallels between play and service were increased by the inclusion of the Sermon at the midway point, the Cathedral setting, and the use of great liturgical passages as links and accompaniments. The emotional structure of the play may be traced in the Choruses, which move from terror and doubts to rapture and a recognition of God's glory. The choices for Thomas and for us are seen from different angles throughout the play. Thomas's moments of decision in Parts I and II are crucial points which cannot be fully presented on stage. In naturalistic terms we have to take Thomas's word for his achievement of true martyrdom; Thomas discovers the impurity of his motives in Part I, while Part II proves that Thomas has virtuously and correctly made his submission to destiny.

(c) The parts of the play

Part One
This Part is constructed in the fashion of a Greek *agon*, or 'verbal conflict', consisting largely of duologues with contributions from a Chorus with a focus on four Temptations. The most dramatic passage presents the surprise Fourth Temptation when Thomas's decision is threatened by self-will and pride. The dramatic centre of the play starts at I.665, 'Now is my way clear', the moment of *peripeteia* when the drama makes a fundamental change in direction. The action of Part I is primarily a matter of mind, the Women of Canterbury full of doubts and fears, while Thomas, having rejected the past, is tempted by his own forward-looking ambitions.

Interlude

The Sermon is a direct, prosaic exposition of the awareness Thomas has attained towards the end of Part I, and it makes clear the nature of his triumph over the Fourth Tempter. It expresses the view that a martyrdom cannot be achieved by man's will alone. It therefore establishes the theme of the play by means of a different dramatic mode. When the future martyr has subdued his own ambitions and will to God's will he becomes a fit instrument for God's purpose. In a cool intellectual fashion it links the poetic sequences of the Parts on either side. Thomas's telling his congregation that he will not preach to them again prepares the way for the events of Part II.

Part Two

The action of this Part contrasts with that of Part I, where we have an internal, intellectual problem followed by a sequence of action and comment. In Part II the focus is murder, and the play generates preparatory emotions: apprehension (Chorus), accusation (Knights), and protection (Priests). The balance of responsibility now becomes important in Thomas's refusal to seek sanctuary. Later, the Knights are to claim that his failure to run amounts to 'suicide', thereby ignoring their own independence as agents of death. In the end the charge is that Thomas should have compromised between the political and religious demands placed upon him; the limited scope of these charges reflects the limitations of the earthly, non-spiritual viewpoint.

Part II expands and embodies the conclusions Thomas himself came to in Part I. Action becomes suffering as he foresaw. If dramatically it lacks development, theatrically it uses bold strokes: priests in procession with banners, the angry intrusion of murderous outsiders, a ritual killing, the great liturgies of *Dies Irae* and *Te Deum*, and the Knights' Shavian Apology in the fashion of the last act of *Saint Joan*.

(d) Linking the parts

Without strict adherence to the Unities of Time and Place the play presents a feeling of a concise Unity of Action. Parts I and II are respectively concerned with the Return and the Murder, but there is a theme common to both Parts, the perception of God's purpose working through an individual and through history. In Part I Thomas the saint comes painfully to his decision; in Part II the time for decision concerns the audience.

Tension is maintained by concentration upon the two phases of Temptation and Murder. In the first the dramatic emphasis concerns Thomas's reappearance at Canterbury, followed by a sequence of choices culminating in the final unexpected temptation. The second phase deals with the expected violence, while the real action traces the Chorus's fears and then the affirmation of their involvement. A second surprise, the Knight's Apology, is reserved for the final movement of the play. Each verse sequence is thus concluded with a prose summary, Sermon and Apology. The humorous tone of the Messenger is balanced by the humour of the Knights, and the Four Tempters grow into and are mirrored by the Four Knights. The tone of the Apology and of the Herald is not the only relief from tension. Other characters besides these examples offer moments of humour throughout the play.

(e) Tragic pattern

The play has the inner structure of a Greek tragedy, and this was traced by Louis Martz in an essay entitled 'The Saint as Tragic Hero' (*Tragic Themes in Western Literature*, ed. Cleanth Brooks). He saw the transfiguration, suffering, the wandering phase, the assertion that the hero will seek no more, and the achievement of peace, acceptance and death in one and the same sanctuary as being derived from the similar elements found in Sophocles's *Oedipus at Colonus*, a play used again by Eliot as the starting-point for his last drama *The Elder Statesman*. But the Christian triumph in the play takes us beyond tragedy. There is a three-fold sequence in Christian self-sacrifice: the Saint first suffers temptation, *pathema*; then detects and resists this temptation, *poiema*; and ultimately gains understanding, *mathema*. The saint derives awareness from his trial sufficient to equip himself for martyrdom.

4.2 CHARACTERISATION

Some critics have claimed that the almost total focus on one main character brought a concentration more suited to a poem than to a play. The other 'lives', it is argued, have no real motivation or individuality, subordinated as they are to Thomas, some speaking only by virtue of his ventriloquism. This line of argument leads to a fundamental rejection of the play as lacking dramatic vitality. To answer such criticism it is appropriate to bear in mind one of the influences suggested by the form of Part I of the play. In the morality play tradition, universal heroes were common, and these were often beset by personalised forces from within themselves. But all Eliot's characters have more intrinsic interest than some critics have allowed.

The groups in *Murder in the Cathedral* are partly medieval – common people, clergy and nobility; they are also reminders of the power groups of 1935, with the ordinary folk squeezed by the confrontation. The characters therefore represent social patterns, each interdependent and in conflict.

All the characters retain an essentially human aspect: the Women of the Chorus bear a burden of age and experience; the Priests are terrified and protective; the Tempters–Knights join in a hideous fellowship; and we enter the thoughts and heart of Thomas at the climax of his life. As people the characters intensify Thomas's spiritual dilemma in a convincingly naturalistic way: the Priests insist on his being their pastoral leader, while the Women react emotionally to his disturbing presence.

The Women and Thomas are linked but contrasted in their response to the assertion of God's purpose, the heroic and extraordinary Saint set off against everyday, suffering humanity. The twin poles of sensibility are revealed, one aware of the spiritual dimension in life, the other unaware and needing enlightenment. In spiritual awareness the lowest level is inhabited by the Tempters and Knights; the Chorus achieve partial awareness; and Thomas attains full understanding.

The Tempters and Knights are linked in significance: Four Tempters tempt Thomas in Part I, while in Part II Four Knights tempt the audience to deny the spiritual truth of Thomas's sacrifice. The representatives of worldly pleasure and political power never understand the central protagonist, and at the close of the play are reiterating their normal everyday vision of life to their own satisfaction. Indeed the minor characters of the play, the Messenger, the Tempters, the Priests, and the Knights, are all largely defined by their function relating to the martyrdom, leading to it, trying to protect, or carrying out the murder. Nevertheless, the characters within each group are carefully individuated.

(a) Thomas

Thomas's earlier life of political power and the fruits of office are presented in retrospect as phases of his present spiritual development. The playwright's concentration upon Thomas's internal debate during his last days brought freshness to what had become a legend. The character of the hero disappointed some critics who saw the characterisation as 'thin' or too symbolic. The spiritual predicament was sometimes appreciated while the personality was rejected as 'flat' or even unconvincing. Other views have exaggerated Thomas's lack of human commitment, and certainly there is little in the play celebratory of the 'good things' of life. Some have called Thomas a 'prig', but such critics mistakenly underestimate the intensity of Thomas's challenge. Conflicts do not necessarily lack force because we have no personal relationships to sustain our interest. Thomas's struggle to overcome his spiritual pride may be an exceptional human experience, but it is seen in dramatic terms, moving through complacency, surprise, humility and courage before the final triumph. Further, the dramatic effectiveness of the play does not diminish when our attention is transferred from the hero's choice to the response of the Chorus. The play is not about the loneliness of the hero; it is about the impact of the hero on everyday life. There is a risk in allowing any character to explore the virtue of his own choices, but Thomas's proud confidence is less priggishness than articulate self-awareness.

Thomas's first temptation involves a rejection of that sensual enjoyment of life which in some measure would seem a normal human indulgence. The second and third temptations are recognised historical and political possibilities facing Thomas then and many people since. But his deliberate setting aside of worldly rewards does not endear him to audiences of a materialist persuasion.

Thomas's confident mockery of the intruders dramatically builds his confidence and pride to the point where the Fourth Temptation becomes personally as well as theatrically real. The emotions in Thomas, the Priests and the Knights are real too. If the world of everyday cares and ambitions is symbolised by the Wheel, then Thomas at the beginning of the action is still subject to its movement. Before the action ends he comes to the 'still point' at the centre of the Wheel, at one with God. Identification with God is a martyr–saint's prerogative, to escape beyond ordinary existence and the compromises of 'living and partly living'. Love, the gratification of the senses, power, politics and the intellectual are superfluous to the single-minded martyr.

The critic Francis Fergusson sees Thomas as a version of the scapegoat of ancient religions, combined with the Sophoclean tragic hero and the Christian martyr–saint. He also sees Thomas as a sort of stage manager, a director of all the climaxes and stage effects central to the play. Thomas is also lecturer, philosopher, theologian and teacher, harshly interpreting reality as vanity in order to achieve a higher plane of understanding.

Lastly, it is possible that the author felt some affinity with his protagonist through their common Christian name. The poet had reaffirmed his Christianity in the Anglican Church only a few years before, and his celebration of the saint confirmed his allegiance. Both poet and hero experienced an absence from their home countries for a number of years, and in both there is a sense of a lonely but triumphant struggle.

(b) The Chorus

This play proves what a useful device the Chorus can be in the modern theatre. In subsequent plays Eliot attempted more concealed versions of the Chorus less successfully. The Chorus has several functions. It contrasts with Thomas's elevated concerns, represents humanity, embodies the theme, acts as commentator and observer, creates mood and atmosphere, and sustains much of the narrative. The affirmative transfiguration of the Chorus in Part II is the true thematic climax of the play.

The Chorus is Greek in form and function, adding to the ritualistic element in the play, but its prominent rôle as an intermediary makes it seem less than stylised. The emotions expressed by the Chorus are a barometer of Thomas's progress. In the end the Women of Canterbury recognise their weakness as a sin, and realise that evil exists but that it may be defeated. Their responses parallel Thomas's experience without his awareness and courage, but without them Thomas would not work out his own crucial decisions. Without Thomas they would put up with tyrannical oppression and settle for a quiet life. At the opening we see that the Women of Canterbury are reluctant to be involved, preferring unobtrusive acceptance of their limited daily round. But the saint compels them to a commitment to faith. The early fears and vacillations make them more human and not less sympathetic. The seasons, the harvests, the problems of everyday life are preferable to the grander challenges involved in the conflict of Archbishop and King. Ultimately they are brought to a recognition that they too are an integral part of the design of human and divine relationships. Their salvation is achieved by witnessing, by nothing more dynamic than being there and saying 'Yes'. Thomas's knowledge of the need for God is transferred to them.

Critics have argued that the Women do not do enough to gain this wisdom for themselves, and do not illuminate their experience with real understanding. They even use Thomas's own language to express their enlightenment at the end. But their joint anonymity enables them to cross the centuries, medieval and modern, representative of the ordinary human level of reality, as well as acting as observers in the fashion of a Greek Chorus. They constitute the touchstone of the play, the past, present and future witnesses of the event. We live through their reactions and participate in the drama through them. In history they represent all humanity faced with an unpalatable and unlooked-for contemporary situation, and in religious terms a development from the compromises of accepting second-best to some identification with Thomas's vision. The journey is conveyed in six long choruses, and their experience is expressed in non-Christian, non-theological terms. It seems excessive to ask for even more dramatically from the Chorus, as if it were possible to incorporate developments more proper to an individual character.

(c) The Priests

The Priests represent an element more contemporarily medieval than the Chorus. They have a rôle to play in Church affairs, subordinate to the Archbishop from whom they gain some understanding of profounder spiritual levels. Their behaviour suggests a pastoral rôle, and sensing the dangers attendant upon the situation they are prepared to take avoiding action.

At the start the Priests are filled with fear, and view their Archbishop's challenging return with caution rather than with zeal. They are closest to Thomas, yet even they are striving for they know not what. They are slow to respond to Thomas's guidance and example, but they come to learn the way forward.

Characterisation, though limited, nevertheless differentiates the three Priests quite clearly. The First Priest is the oldest of the three, equable, easy-going and kindly. The Second Priest is more assertive and eager, a younger cleric anxious to prove his loyalty. The Third Priest is the quietest of the three, meditative, more profound in his religious commitment, and it is he who assesses the Knights for us.

(d) Tempters and Knights

Becket realises his divine destiny at the expense of human identity, and the further he moves away by resisting temptation the more remote he apparently becomes in the eyes of ordinary people. But *his* temptations give way to *ours* so that the necessities of this world are amusingly and powerfully embodied first by the Tempters and subsequently by the Knights. The shared impulse to challenge and tempt makes the playing of the two quartets by the same actors sensible and meaningful. The Knights recapitulate the spirit and logic of the Tempters, and the two groups are linked by tone and motivation. The First Tempter has a commitment to life at its immediate and physical level, and offering no reasons beyond sensual enjoyment and the good things of life he can only act as Chairman for the Knights. The Second Tempter offers temporal power on behalf of good causes, and has no wish to alter the social pattern, being quite willing to make his way within the established order; as Knight he justifies the murder as securing 'social justice'. The Third Tempter argues for rebellion to defeat the King's autocracy, and sets out to achieve a radical re-structuring and subsequent change; as Knight then he is able to argue his own individual disinterestedness. The Fourth Tempter is different in kind from the others, an egotistical assertion of Thomas's own spiritual pride; he will embrace martyrdom to achieve spiritual power over mankind for ever. As a Knight he argues that Thomas embraced his own fate, and that this consti-tuted suicide.

The Tempters

Thematically the first three Tempters represent a denial of the life of the spirit and so they stress Thomas's personal and political status. In their eyes the Church is power, not spirit, and the Knights continue this pressure on the hero, demanding that he accept *this* world's sovereignty. The first three Temptations, worldly pleasures, alliance with the King, and alliance against the King, constitute an exposition of the past, and it has been argued that because they retell what has happened already their contribution lacks dramatic force. Stephen Spender in his Fontana Modern Masters book on Eliot has also commented on the ease with which Thomas dismisses the first three Temptations, and he sees them more as embarrassing ghosts in the fashion of the figures from the past in *The Elder Statesman*. Thomas is haunted by these 'urgings', as well as tempted, and this makes the interaction between hero and Tempters highly dramatic.

Drama uses many methods of revealing a character's heart-searching. *Hamlet* has a series of soliloquies; Arthur Miller uses flashbacks in *Death of a Salesman*; Eliot creates allegorical impersonations in the medieval fashion to project the four Temptations. It is mistaken to make too much of E. Martin Browne's comment that we should see the Temptations as 'figments' of Thomas's imagination. They are imagined in one sense, but morality play figures have a complex life, combining both inner and outer characteristics. The Tempters mark the stages of Thomas's purification with challenges of great variety and enjoyable vivacity.

The First Tempter: The favouritism of the King had ensured Thomas's full indulgence in the good life, the sweets of office, the perquisites of being one of the important people. *L'homme moyen sensuel* comes into his own. The Tempter urges Thomas to take what the world offers to those blessed with favour. At worst sensuality or at best high living would be attractive to most of the audience, but they are also forced to realise that the First Tempter is telling Thomas to take the easy way out and not to mind responsibilities. Denial is made easy for Thomas because this Temptation looks back to a life he has long left behind.

The Second Tempter: This Temptation is more cunningly provoking to Thomas than is often considered. The renewal of friendship with the King and the assumption of the Chancellorship would allow Thomas to do a great deal for suffering humanity. It is the subtlest of the first three Temptations, since the wielding of temporal power is given a Christian twist:

> Rule for the good of the better cause.

This is a carefully judged challenge, for the Tempter is arguing that Thomas has only to give way on a minor point in order to achieve virtuous objectives:

> Real power
> Is purchased at price of a certain submission.

Several twentieth-century problems are hinted at here: the relationship of the individual to the State, the balance between Church and Government power and, above all, the need to undertake dubious projects for laudable ends.

The Third Tempter: The Third Tempter offers another version of temporal power, a combination of Church and People to overthrow tyranny. Thomas still speaks as a loyal subject and condemns an alliance of factions against central authority, however 'popular' the rebellion may be. This, then, is the least engaging of the Temptations, since it offers only political manoeuvres in a struggle for power. If Thomas has overcome the Temptation of worldly power for good he is hardly likely to ally himself with the self-interested barons. The machinations of a new coalition leading to insurrection against the King are rejected by a man who has accepted the higher authority of God.

The Fourth Tempter: The Fourth Temptation is less a shadowy assault from external forces, a 'haunting' from the past, than a Mephistopheles working through a man's most vulnerable weakness to gain evil possession. Seemingly the would-be martyr cannot achieve glory without sin. This Tempter is a terrifying mirror image of Thomas himself, a creature relishing the consequences of martyrdom. The Fourth Tempter is the False Thomas. Spiritual aspiration confronts him insidiously with a sinful version of his own desires. Thomas's celebration of his own superior knowledge of suffering and action is revealed as tainted by the Tempter's mockery. Spiritual pride is now seen to be a trap. The elucidation of this Temptation is found in Thomas's Sermon.

The Knights
The Knights have a group identity, a comic burlesque act. Each has an individual style rather than differentiation of character. They are a gang of murderers, killing out of policy which gives them a bloodthirsty drive without personal motivation. They do not matter as people, revealing the dedicated brutality of a totalitarian state of the 1930s. The deed seems less the murder of a man by other men than a symbolic, ritual act, although Eliot does give them names in the Apology. Their lack of personality and of personal feelings and their subjugation to ideas makes a point about the possibility of men losing their humanity.

One of the great novelties of the play is the introduction of a clever satire after the stylised murder. Ashley Dukes of the Mercury Theatre warned against allowing the Knights' Apology to become comic in an obvious way. They take themselves seriously, and for all their unconscious humour they are still instruments of evil.

The Knights, in effect, argue that the Church should subordinate itself to the secular powers of the State. In advancing their various arguments in the Apology the Knights reveal their dramatic and thematic link to the Tempters in Part I. It is the audience who are being tempted now, asked to accept the worldy viewpoint implicit in the Knights' versions of Thomas's death. Ironically, despite their belief in their chosen course of action they too serve God's purpose; in taking 'action' they 'suffer' an all-powerful design.

4.3 VERSE DRAMA

(a) The choice of verse

The prime justification for using verse in drama is that it will achieve more than prose. In 1936 Eliot claimed that verse drama gave a more complete experience than the 'abstraction' of prose, implying that the dialogue of the latter communicated only at a simple level. The playwright should not think of poetry as something added. Verse enabled him to orchestrate the drama like a piece of music. Action and plot captivate audiences, but they should also be moved by a pattern underlying plot where deeper, non-articulated levels of feeling may be tapped. Verse forms, rhythms, language and imagery intensify dramatic situation, dialogue and motivation.

Another poet, Christopher Hassall, noted later in 1948 that playwrights had become dissatisfied with the surface of things, and so realistic character and action were seen as inadequate pictures. Verse and language were to provide the means for deeper interpretations of life. Eliot reviewed his 1935 choices in his essay 'Poetry and Drama' (1951). Obviously in *Murder in the Cathedral* he could not use the language of the twelfth century, either Anglo-Saxon or Norman French. The language had to be lively enough to concentrate the attention of a modern audience and yet convincing enough to take them back to a distant historical event. Since he wanted to draw a contemporary moral from the material the last effect he wanted was an archaic distancing. Eliot felt he had to avoid the Shakespearean echo which had dogged nineteenth-century verse dramatists, largely attributable in Eliot's view to the use of iambic pentameter blank verse. The basic verse form Eliot adopted was that of *Everyman*, the English morality play, which offered the additionally useful effects of alliteration and occasional rhyme. The most prominent metre in Eliot's play is a four-stress line, building up through similar, parallel units of contrasting or balanced phrasing bound together by alliteration (I. 364–7).

This effect is a development of one employed by Eliot in his earlier poems like 'The Waste Land'. The colloquial and poetic are interwoven to create tension between spiritual awareness and everyday realities.

Changes of rhythm prepare listeners for each new kind of response or variation in emotion. The First Tempter's lightly tripping abstractions contrast with the heavier kind found in Thomas's anticipatory 'For a little time the hungry hawk' speech (I. 255–9). Couplets with double rhymes produce emphasis, derision and aggression. A different kind of emphasis comes from the Third Tempter's removal of the definite article from his summary of the political situation, giving it the air of an irrefutable proposition which is quite spurious. The tetrameters are forceful and insistent.

Long lines precede shorter ones, as in the opening contrast between the broad poetic movements of the Chorus's questioning of their unease, and the agitated repetitions of the Priests' (I. 42–8, 51–2).

The play is enriched by the development of echoes and repetitions which bind and advance interpretative meaning in a challenging way. The most significant and extended example of the technique is found in the Fourth Tempter's parody of Thomas's centrally important first speech (I. 207–17 and 591–9). In contrast to the Tempter's mockery of Thomas's confident abstractions the Chorus use longer lines descriptive of an everyday reality given a nightmare quality (I. 600–1).

The intellectual challenge of the Tempter is intensified by the sensuous vividness of the alarm of the Women, by the simple, direct language and flatness of tone; a thoughtful formality is immediately matched by images from daily life. Yet even the key profundities of the 'You know and do not know' passage become a refrain that catches the ear because of and in spite of the intricate phrasing. The variously exciting modes of verse are interesting in themselves, but they are also significantly appropriate to speaker and subject matter. Eliot makes verse and imagery serve his dramatic purpose. The simple doggerel of the Knights in unison presents their united intention and their lack of separate personalities (II. 353–6).

Like the Old Vice, a farcical attendant upon the Devil in the medieval morality plays, the vulgar Knights at times are presented humorously in the exaggerated terms of comic variety theatre; at other times they assume the spurious *bonhomie* of the hustings or political rally. The colloquial Apology deliberately breaks the surface of the play, and this seems to have posed problems for some critics. The Apology acts in the fashion of Brechtian 'alienation', shocking for a purpose, to distance the audience from their emotional response to the preceding action.

Rhyming tetrameters are used to pose Thomas's retorts to the Tempters' taunts, and couplets abound (I. 461–4). Thomas responds to the agonised Chorus with resolute propositions rhymed neatly in couplets:

Now is my way clear, now is the meaning plain;
Temptation shall not come in this kind again.
The last temptation is the greatest treason:
To do the right deed for the wrong reason. (I. 665–8)

The verse of the Chorus is the most varied, reflecting its many purposes. Free flowing lines of different lengths build atmospheric description (I. 9–11). A more insistent rhythm emphasises the natures of the daily round (I. 31–3). Beneath the familiar there is unease. The longest lines reflect panic, the repetition of powerful verbs adding to the terror (II. 422). Passages of powerful emotion are counterpointed with liturgy, the *Te Deum* (II. 618–50) and the *Dies Irae* (II. 279–309), while introits accompany the processional opening of Part II.

In such a variety of effects lay part of Eliot's hope that verse would achieve more than prose. He showed too that he could differentiate character in verse. The Tempters, for instance, use a kind of clipped economy of expression which gives their lines a common challenging tone, and yet they are also established as individuals. The First Tempter is characterised by flights of lyrical poetry; the Second Tempter's emphatic tone derives from an insistently rhythmic verse full of alliteration; the Third Tempter's favoured 'man to man' approach is helped by colloquial intonation; and the Fourth parodies Thomas's own voice and language.

Unadorned the verse can be realistically descriptive, as in the Messenger's account of the people's welcome to Thomas on his return (I. 88–90). Here Eliot is at his most Shakespearean. Other passages are suitably realistic, as in the description of merchant and labourer (I. 27–8). Homely realism rapidly but smoothly gravitates to the elevated questioning of fear and doubt (I. 36–9). When the Tempters combine in their own chorus towards the end of Part I the short lines of abstractions lead to lists of endeavour and effort which are mocked as meaningless (I. 605–10). Questions give simple happenings a threatening effect in a single long line describing rain and wind (I. 626). Long lines also elevate humble actions in the final affirmation (II. 625).

Prose is used to bring the play back to our world, down to earth, in the Apology and the Sermon, both of them adopting public forms of address, defensive and threatening in the former, intimate and interpretative in the latter. A sermon is exactly right in terms of the play's setting and hero, and also corresponds usefully to the dramatic device of the soliloquy. The prose give audiences' ears a pause from the insistent and powerful rhythms of the verse, and offers explanations, one true and one false, of the central event.

(b) Imagery

Symbols and images echo throughout the play, and in the Choruses these move from negative caution and fearfulness to positive affirmation. The imagery of the Tempters in Part I is medieval, while in Part II the Knights bring us into the modern world. The varied styles and references involve our consciousness in past, present and future, range over childhood, maturity and death, and probe both the lower depths of fears and dreams and the heights of ecstatic joy.

Seasonal imagery, mainly wintry, dominates the play, creating an atmosphere of foreboding, death, darkness and despair. The seasonal setting becomes a metaphor for spiritual deprivation, and states of mind match the shrinking senses beset by winter. The colours are subdued:

Evil the wind, and bitter the sea, and grey the sky, grey grey grey.
(I. 147)

The surface reflects the anguish beneath. Eliot uses images of 'unnatural' Nature which featured in his earlier poetry. The Chorus are half-hearted in their participation in seasonal change in the opening of the play; only at the end are the breadth of landscape, the seasonal cycle, and domestic harmony restored to their natural order.

The animal references in the play recall a medieval bestiary, but they convey a modern message. Eliot uses them to express rejection, horror and evil. The imagery of undersea life as a kind of living death again reminds us of earlier Eliot poetry. The repetitive addition of the prefix 'jack' to three of the animals, 'jackal, jackass, jackdaw' creates a feeling of contempt. The movements are repulsive – 'twisting' and 'turning'. In this oblique fashion Eliot introduces a sense of sin to a partially comprehending modern audience.

The most important images aimed at communicating a Christian view of life are the linked ideas of the Wheel and the 'still point'. The whole concept represents the created world with God at the centre. Mankind moves at the circumference, apparently free, but the real control and focus of the movement of the Wheel remains at the 'still centre', God incarnate.

(c) Dramatic styles

The description of the play as 'verse drama' is too simple. In the Knights we have the melodrama of the murder, a music-hall turn in the comic aspects of their Apology, and Shavian farce in their shock assumption of modern attitudes. As a religious experience it offers the liturgy of the *Dies Irae*, the *Te Deum*, introits and versicles. In the focus on Thomas we have a 'biblical' presentation on the scale of the Book of Job, a mystery play in the story of a saint, a derivative from Milton's *Samson Agonistes*, with a central figure beset by Tempters, and a modern morality play reminiscent of *Everyman*, featuring a central protagonist confronted by a sequence of allegorical personages.

The Chorus are not the only reminder of Greek drama. Critics have pointed to the Aeschylean nature of the play, a primitive tragedy concentrating on a single event and a single hero, both observed from different angles of vision while tension and suspense steadily increase. The influence of *The Rock* upon the writing of this play may have been underestimated. The pageant form had a particularly strong fascination for English audiences between the two world wars, and its traditional celebration of key episodes in English history reminds us of both *The Rock* and *Murder in the Cathedral*.

The idea that the play lacks roots seems absurd; rather, it might be seen to have too many. For Eliot, safeguarding a living theatre meant tapping established traditions. The strands interwoven into the play's texture range over the centuries, and few of them presented the kind of life associated with naturalism. Eliot's play is not a drama of human relationships, although there is real terror in the reactions of Chorus and Priests to portentous events. In part it is a symbolic play of ideas in its portrayal of man's struggle with sin and temptation, and its plot has the careful organisation and balance of a Ben Jonson play. *Murder in the Cathedral* is a theatrical *tour de force*.

5 SPECIMEN PASSAGE

AND

COMMENTARY

THOMAS
Is there no way, in my soul's sickness,
Does not lead to damnation in pride?
I well know that these temptations
Mean present vanity and future torment.
Can sinful pride be driven out
Only by more sinful? Can I neither act nor suffer
Without perdition?   590

TEMPTER
You know and do not know, what it is to act or suffer.
You know and do not know, that action is suffering,
And suffering action. Neither does the agent suffer
Nor the patient act. But both are fixed
In an eternal action, an eternal patience
To which all must consent that it may be willed
And which all must suffer that they may will it,
That the pattern may subsist, that the wheel may turn and
  still
Be forever still.

CHORUS
There is no rest in the house. There is no rest in the street.   600
I hear restless movement of feet. And the air is heavy and
  thick.
Thick and heavy the sky. And the earth presses up against
  our feet.

What is the sickly smell, the vapour? The dark green light
   from a cloud on a withered tree? The earth is heaving
   to parturition of issue of hell. What is the sticky dew
   that forms on the back of my hand?

THE FOUR TEMPTERS
Man's life is a cheat and a disappointment;
All things are unreal,
Unreal or disappointing:
The Catherine wheel, the pantomime cat,
The prizes given at the children's party,
The prize awarded for the English Essay,
The scholar's degree, the statesman's decoration.   610
All things become less real, man passes
From unreality to unreality.
This man is obstinate, blind, intent
On self-destruction,
Passing from deception to deception,
From grandeur to grandeur to final illusion,
Lost in the wonder of his own greatness,
The enemy of society, enemy of himself. (I. 584–618)

Thomas has dealt confidently with the first three Temptations, but
has been surprised by a fourth challenge urging him to follow his
own desires and seek martyrdom. He has the salutory experience
of discovering his heartfelt ambitions to be sinful; his ambitions
must be purged of self. The Fourth Tempter destroys Thomas's
confidence by adapting the Archbishop's first assertion in mocking
fashion. The Four Tempters in unison follow up their destructive
advantage by calling in doubt all ambitions and rewards.

   This passage builds up to one of the great climaxes of the play. It
demonstrates a variety of verse styles, full of tension and contrasts.
It shows how the elements of the drama combine: the protagonist,
the forces acting upon him, and the emotional response of the
Chorus. A switchback sequence of effects keeps the audience on
their toes, and four emotions are engendered in rapid succession – bewilderment, mockery, anxiety, sneering derision. Abstractions dominate the language of Thomas and the Fourth
Tempter; a sensuous nightmare occupies the Chorus; and this
contrasts with the worldly catalogue of the Tempters in chorus,

who return to abstractions when they focus again on Thomas alone.

Agitation in Thomas takes the form of questioning his own pride; agitation in the Chorus is seen as an awareness of perverted nature. The Tempters probe and intensify the agony. They assert; Thomas and the Chorus ask questions. The Chorus's free verse lines lengthen to match their mounting distress, particularly their last line (603), which is as long as four normal lines.

The passage shows the poet's skill in adapting the four-stress line freely to his varied dramatic purposes. The beat heavily reinforces the questioning verbs (I. 584–90), 'Is', 'Does' and 'Can'. The four stresses also bring out the obsessive exploration of the key words:

> You knów and do not knów, what it is to áct or súffer.
> You knów and do not knów, that áction is súffering,
> And súffering áction. (I. 591–3)

The metre fits question, statement and then the dismissive catalogue of the Tempters in chorus:

> The Cátherine whéel, the pántomime cát.
> The prízes gíven at the chíldren's párty,
> The príze awárded for the English Eśsay,
> The schólar's degrée, the státesman's décoration. (I. 607–10)

Thomas's quandary is described in lines 584–90. Must his spiritual ambition lead to sin? It leads into his moments of maximum weakness and vulnerability. Lines 591–9 show how the repetition of his own words (208–17) intensifies the surprise, and in the repetition the tone changes from confidence to confusion, from bold resolution to awareness of sinful error.

The central emphasis here is upon the fixed implacability of fate; Thomas has merely to succumb to a pre-ordained destiny. Thomas's more positive phrase 'for the pattern is the action/And the suffering' is omitted by the Fourth Tempter. An act undertaken for human motives lacks moral certainties; an act matching God's will resolves problems of good and evil. Thomas is in danger of acting to make the Wheel turn to his desires instead of allowing God at the 'still centre' to provide the motive power. In lines 600–3 the lengthening lines convey a steadily intensifying disquiet, and the imagery portrays a reversal of the natural order. On this occasion the Chorus act as a prologue to a combined sequence involving all three groups outside Thomas himself. Lines 604–18 show the Tempters reflecting criticism of Thomas's rejection of worldly rewards; life is celebrated as a disappointment. Thomas seeks to rise above the world of transitory satisfactions, and the Tempters offer us images of rewards giving less than they promised. The arbitrary list makes them seem trivial, and the items are linked by rhymes and echoes, 'Cath/cat' and repeated 'prizes'. The Tempters misinterpret Thomas's silence and wrongly anticipate his succumbing to the Fourth Temptation, 'Lost in the wonder of his own greatness'.

The Tempters' own chorus is followed by the Chorus's growing agitation. Thomas's isolation is emphasised by the combination of Tempters, Priests and Chorus alternately expressing menace and doubt. Thomas alone is prepared for a decision, and at the moment the Chorus are still in the situation of begging Thomas to save himself, he has a new confidence: 'Now is my way clear'. The Chorus sense the danger but cannot find the cause of cure. They prefer to go on 'Living and partly living.'

6 CRITICAL RECEPTION

Some early reviews were welcoming; others were dismissive. Rayner Heppenstall liked several things: the realistic presentation of the Devil, the super-Shavian purgative humour, and three or four pieces of superb liturgical incantation. *The Times Literary Supplement* considered the play a successful combination and stressed its ritualistic aspects without ever admitting it had theatrical potential: 'This is his most unified writing. He has admirably brought to maturity his long experimenting for a dramatic style, the chief merit of which lies in his writing for a chorus.' Others thought it was a clever combination but felt it was cold and academic. Mark Van Doren considered it 'thin' too, because he claimed theology always made for 'thin' drama, but saw the play as a masterpiece full of ironies. Ashley Dukes and friends were concerned to encourage the growth of a poetic drama, and noted the 180 Mercury Theatre performances and the fact that one in twenty from the audiences actually bought the text. In fact, most of those in favour of the play saw it as the forerunner of a new kind of drama. Michael Roberts saw Thomas as the successful mediator between sainthood and the audience as Eliot intended.

Contrary critics tended to look for 'dramatic faults'. John Crowe Ransom, for instance, thought Eliot should have done without prose, and pointed to the naming of the Knights after their namelessness as an error. Michael Sayers led a more formidable opposition, dismissing the 'desiccated' poetry, the 'static exhibition' of the action, and its content which 'repudiates all the popular values in life and theatre of our time'. Kenneth Allott, in reviewing *The Dog Beneath the Skin*, comically forecast *The*

Family Reunion without realising it by describing *Murder in the Cathedral* as 'country house charades performed by elderly rheumatic folk'. The strength of Allott's animosity was surprising considering the evident impact of the play upon early audiences. More specific charges concerned the supposed 'undramatic' qualities of the play. Horace Gregory described the action as 'abruptly frozen in mid-air', while Louis MacNeice felt it was only 'nearly a play' because 'it is a foregone conclusion and a foregone conclusion is not dramatic'. These criticisms tend to ignore the play's novelty in form and to demand of it qualities which are to be found in other kinds of plays. Eliot's Christian stance was unacceptable to some critics, although an inability to share an author's belief ought not to lead to uncritical rejection of a play.

Carping criticism continued in the post-war period following years of successful production. John Middleton Murry in 1956 was one of the few to see no contemporary relevance in the play, claiming it was too far from the human condition. Francis Fergusson was similarly critical of Eliot's remoteness from everyday life, although the American Federal Theater production proved to him that the play could be 'very effective theatrically'. Eric Bentley ruefully observed that it was 'almost ostentatiously stageworthy', and J. C. Trewin seemed an equally reluctant convert: 'In the theatre it can grow upon one.'

Steadily, however, the play's regular appearance in the national repertoire further established its reputation, and Raymond Williams has pinpointed the nature of its success: 'It has a completeness which springs from the perfect matching of material and form.' As a forerunner of a great new dramatic movement it may have been a disappointment to Eliot's faithful producer, E. Martin Browne, who nevertheless saw it as 'the one acknowledged masterpiece to have come out of the modern verse-play revival'.

The reputation of the play seems stable now, and it is frequently revived. The majority view appears to be that Eliot matched form to theme and occasion, that he created something unique, and that the play is his theatrical masterpiece. Contrary views attacking the 'faulty' or 'undramatic' form of the play, asserting that it does not fit the profiles of established dramatic forms, that because most of the conflict in Part I is internalised there is no action, or that the use of prose shows that the poet could not keep up the poetry all of the time, lack critical force.

Eliot was only too aware himself of the remoteness from contemporary experience of concepts like martyrdom, sin and divine grace. The play purports to define these ideas for us afresh, and continuing productions show that people are still eager to experience the dramatisation of those definitions.

_____ was unable to trace any sample of the material _____ conditions of work, to compare the various sam- _____ given price. The physical basis of the theory, therefore, is fresh ____ and beautiful production theory that stresses _____ small num- _____ that are important in the economic process.

7 THE MODERN VERSE MOVEMENT

The impetus towards a modern verse drama grew out of two approaches to the solution of contemporary problems; one was political and the other was religious. Plays with a pre-war political message and Eliot's *Sweeney Agonistes* owed much to European expressionism, a movement critical of the existing social order, and more concerned to explore psychological states than to portray life realistically. Eliot's plays from *The Rock* onwards and the religious verse-plays by other poets looked more to English forms as models.

Modern verse dramatists saw it as their task to theorise about the form, to create viable pieces for theatrical production, and to encourage an audience for their drama. An intense discussion in literary magazines preceded the appearance of *Murder in the Cathedral*. The major problem identified by most poet-dramatists was the language; modern verse drama had to have the right sort of speech. Others urged either that action was of prime importance or that it was wrong to worry about there being too much imagery or too great a dependence upon blank verse. The main drift of the supportive debate was the notion that prose as a medium in naturalistic drama limits expression and subtlety. Most poet-dramatists agreed that poetry had not to be mere decoration, and that it was wrong if the listener dwelt upon the poetry. The first important achievement was to make the audience respond to the action and to the characters through the poetry. Further, both religious and political poet-dramatists saw the medium as capable of exploring profounder levels of human experience.

Eliot was both pioneer and the 'leader' of the movement. His contribution was the most substantial and enduring. From *Sweeney Agonistes* to *The Elder Statesman* Eliot's effort spanned thirty years. W. H. Auden proceeded on a parallel path, combining with Christopher Isherwood to write several plays, the best known of which, *The Ascent of F6*, was considered one of the progeny of *Murder in the Cathedral*, although it explored political and social awareness rather than a religious dilemma.

Christopher Fry was the only poet-dramatist to equal Eliot's output, both pre-war and post-war and, for a time, to match his success, notably with his comedies of the late forties like *The Lady's Not For Burning*. Eliot's success in *Murder in the Cathedral* encouraged derivative works inspired by a Christian message, like Ronald Duncan's *This Way to the Tomb*, but Fry's deliberate display or pyrotechnic language was a departure from Eliot's post-war search for a less 'poetic' verse. The most successful play of this later Eliot period was *The Cocktail Party*.

Murder in the Cathedral did not solve the general problems of writing a modern verse drama (see sections 1.2 and 1.4), but neither did its successors, because in the fifties British drama changed direction towards a more prosaic realism, exploring 'kitchen sink' themes and social commitment. But despite changes in theatrical fashion both *Murder in the Cathedral* and *The Cocktail Party* enjoy continued revivals.

REVISION QUESTIONS

1. Each part of *Murder in the Cathedral* deals with a different kind of action. Which action is more 'real' or more important to the play?

2. 'The greatest success in *Murder in the Cathedral* lies in its Choruses, where Eliot provided the best poetry.' Discuss.

3. Discuss Eliot's presentation of martyrdom and martyr in *Murder in the Cathedral*.

4. 'Who killed the Archbishop?' Discuss the dramatic effectiveness and significance of the Knights' Apology after the murder.

5. Discuss the view that Becket is more successful as a vehicle of the author's ideas than as a character.

6. Eliot stated that religious plays had to provide 'ordinary dramatic interest'. To what extent does *Murder in the Cathedral* combine both religious and 'ordinary dramatic interest' successfully?

7. Eliot claimed that the use of poetry in drama could be justified only if it achieved more than prose. What positive functions does the poetry have in *Murder in the Cathedral*?

8. What methods does Eliot use to make the twelfth century relevant to the twentieth?

9. Early critics saw *Murder in the Cathedral* as a modern tragedy. In what ways does the play conform to your idea of a tragedy?

10. Show how Eliot uses a variety of dramatic techniques in the presentation of his themes in *Murder in the Cathedral*.

11. Discuss the view that Thomas is the only developed character in *Murder in the Cathedral*.
12. Critics have disagreed about the success of *Murder in the Cathedral* as a drama. What is your own view?

FURTHER READING

T. S. Eliot

'The Possibility of a Poetic Drama', *The Sacred Wood* (1920).
'A Dialogue on Dramatic Poetry' (1928), *Selected Essays* (1932).
'Poetry and Drama' (1951), *On Poetry and Poets* (1957).

Critical works

Browne, E. Martin (1969), *The Making of T. S. Eliot's Plays* (Cambridge University Press, London, pp. 34–89).
Gardner, Helen (1949), 'The Language of Drama', *The Art of T. S. Eliot* (Cresset, London, pp. 133–9).
Hinchliffe, A. P. (1985), 'Murder in the Cathedral', *T. S. Eliot: Plays* (Macmillan Casebook, London, pp. 88–117).
Jones, D. E. (1960), *The Plays of T. S. Eliot* (Routledge and Kegan Paul, London, pp. 50–81).
Matthiessen, F. O. (1958), *The Achievement of T. S. Eliot* (Oxford University Press, London, pp. 162–5, 171–4).
Pickering, K. (1985), 'Murder in the Cathedral', *Drama in the Cathedral* (Churchman, Worthing, pp. 178–95).
Smith, Carol H. (1963), '*The Rock* and *Murder in the Cathedral*', *T. S. Eliot's Dramatic Theory and Practice* (Oxford University Press, London, pp. 76–111).
Weales, Gerald (1961), 'T. S. Eliot and Christopher Fry', *Religion in Modern English Drama* (University of Pennsylvania Press, Philadelphia, pp. 183–225).

Mastering English Literature

Richard Gill

Mastering English Literature will help readers both to enjoy English Literature and to be successful in 'O' levels, 'A' levels and other public exams. It is an introduction to the study of poetry, novels and drama which helps the reader in four ways – by providing ways of approaching literature, by giving examples and practice exercises, by offering hints on how to write about literature, and by the author's own evident enthusiasm for the subject. With extracts from more than 200 texts, this is an enjoyable account of how to get the maximum satisfaction out of reading, whether it be for formal examinations or simply for pleasure.

Work Out English Literature ('A' level)

S.H. Burton

This book familiarises 'A' level English Literature candidates with every kind of test which they are likely to encounter. Suggested answers are worked out step by step and accompanied by full author's commentary. The book helps students to clarify their aims and establish techniques and standards so that they can make appropriate responses to similar questions when the examination pressures are on. It opens up fresh ways of looking at the full range of set texts, authors and critical judgements and motivates students to know more of these matters.

Also from Macmillan

CASEBOOK SERIES

The Macmillan *Casebook* series brings together the best of modern criticism with a selection of early reviews and comments. Each Casebook charts the development of opinion on a play, poem, or novel, or on a literary genre, from its first appearance to the present day.

GENERAL THEMES

COMEDY: DEVELOPMENTS IN CRITICISM
D. J. Palmer

DRAMA CRITICISM: DEVELOPMENTS SINCE IBSEN
A. J. Hinchliffe

THE ENGLISH NOVEL: DEVELOPMENTS IN CRITICISM SINCE HENRY JAMES
Stephen Hazell

THE LANGUAGE OF LITERATURE
N. Page

THE PASTORAL MODE
Bryan Loughrey

THE ROMANTIC IMAGINATION
J. S. Hill

TRAGEDY: DEVELOPMENTS IN CRITICISM
R. P. Draper

POETRY

WILLIAM BLAKE: SONGS OF INNOCENCE AND EXPERIENCE
Margaret Bottrall

BROWNING: MEN AND WOMEN AND OTHER POEMS
J. R. Watson

BYRON: CHILDE HAROLD'S PILGRIMAGE AND DON JUAN
John Jump

CHAUCER: THE CANTERBURY TALES
J. J. Anderson

COLERIDGE: THE ANCIENT MARINER AND OTHER POEMS
A. R. Jones and W. Tydeman

DONNE: SONGS AND SONETS
Julian Lovelock

T. S. ELIOT: FOUR QUARTETS
Bernard Bergonzi

T. S. ELIOT: PRUFROCK, GERONTION, ASH WEDNESDAY AND OTHER POEMS
B. C. Southam

T. S. ELIOT: THE WASTELAND
C. B. Cox and A. J. Hinchliffe

ELIZABETHAN POETRY: LYRICAL AND NARRATIVE
Gerald Hammond

THOMAS HARDY: POEMS
J. Gibson and T. Johnson

GERALD MANLEY HOPKINS: POEMS
Margaret Bottrall

KEATS: ODES
G. S. Fraser

KEATS: THE NARRATIVE POEMS
J. S. Hill

MARVELL: POEMS
Arthur Pollard

THE METAPHYSICAL POETS
Gerald Hammond

MILTON: PARADISE LOST
A. E. Dyson and Julian Lovelock

POETRY OF THE FIRST WORLD
WAR
Dominic Hibberd

ALEXANDER POPE: THE RAPE OF
THE LOCK
John Dixon Hunt

SHELLEY: SHORTER POEMS &
LYRICS
Patrick Swinden

SPENSER: THE FAERIE QUEEN
Peter Bayley

TENNYSON: IN MEMORIAM
John Dixon Hunt

THIRTIES POETS: 'THE AUDEN
GROUP'
Ronald Carter

WORDSWORTH: LYRICAL
BALLADS
A. R. Jones and W. Tydeman

WORDSWORTH: THE PRELUDE
W. J. Harvey and R. Gravil

W. B. YEATS: POEMS 1919–1935
E. Cullingford

W. B. YEATS: LAST POEMS
Jon Stallworthy

THE NOVEL AND PROSE

JANE AUSTEN: EMMA
David Lodge

JANE AUSTEN: NORTHANGER
ABBEY AND PERSUASION
B. C. Southam

JANE AUSTEN: SENSE AND
SENSIBILITY, PRIDE AND
PREJUDICE AND MANSFIELD
PARK
B. C. Southam

CHARLOTTE BRONTË: JANE EYRE
AND VILLETTE
Miriam Allott

EMILY BRONTË: WUTHERING
HEIGHTS
Miriam Allott

BUNYAN: THE PILGRIM'S
PROGRESS
R. Sharrock

CONRAD: HEART OF DARKNESS,
NOSTROMO AND UNDER
WESTERN EYES
C. B. Cox

CONRAD: THE SECRET AGENT
Ian Watt

CHARLES DICKENS: BLEAK
HOUSE
A. E. Dyson

CHARLES DICKENS: DOMBEY
AND SON AND LITTLE DORRITT
Alan Shelston

CHARLES DICKENS: HARD TIMES,
GREAT EXPECTATIONS AND OUR
MUTUAL FRIEND
N. Page

GEORGE ELIOT: MIDDLEMARCH
Patrick Swinden

GEORGE ELIOT: THE MILL ON
THE FLOSS AND SILAS MARNER
R. P. Draper

HENRY FIELDING: TOM JONES
Neil Compton

E. M. FORSTER: A PASSAGE TO
INDIA
Malcolm Bradbury

HARDY: THE TRAGIC NOVELS
R. P. Draper

HENRY JAMES: WASHINGTON
SQUARE AND THE PORTRAIT OF
A LADY
Alan Shelston

JAMES JOYCE: DUBLINERS AND A
PORTRAIT OF THE ARTIST AS A
YOUNG MAN
Morris Beja

D. H. LAWRENCE: THE RAINBOW
AND WOMEN IN LOVE
Colin Clarke

D. H. LAWRENCE: SONS AND
LOVERS
Gamini Salgado

SWIFT: GULLIVER'S TRAVELS
Richard Gravil

THACKERAY: VANITY FAIR
Arthur Pollard

TROLLOPE: THE BARSETSHIRE
NOVELS
T. Bareham

VIRGINIA WOOLF: TO THE
LIGHTHOUSE
Morris Beja

DRAMA

CONGREVE: COMEDIES
Patrick Lyons

T. S. ELIOT: PLAYS
Arnold P. Hinchliffe

JONSON: EVERY MAN IN HIS
HUMOUR AND THE ALCHEMIST
R. V. Holdsworth

JONSON: VOLPONE
J. A. Barish

MARLOWE: DR FAUSTUS
John Jump

MARLOWE: TAMBURLAINE,
EDWARD II AND THE JEW OF
MALTA
John Russell Brown

MEDIEVAL ENGLISH DRAMA
Peter Happé

O'CASEY: JUNO AND THE
PAYCOCK, THE PLOUGH AND THE
STARS AND THE SHADOW OF A
GUNMAN
R. Ayling

JOHN OSBORNE: LOOK BACK IN
ANGER
John Russell Taylor

WEBSTER: THE WHITE DEVIL AND
THE DUCHESS OF MALFI
R. V. Holdsworth

WILDE: COMEDIES
W. Tydeman

SHAKESPEARE

SHAKESPEARE: ANTONY AND
CLEOPATRA
John Russell Brown

SHAKESPEARE: CORIOLANUS
B. A. Brockman

SHAKESPEARE: HAMLET
John Jump

SHAKESPEARE: HENRY IV PARTS
I AND II
G. K. Hunter

SHAKESPEARE: HENRY V
Michael Quinn

SHAKESPEARE: JULIUS CAESAR
Peter Ure

SHAKESPEARE: KING LEAR
Frank Kermode

SHAKESPEARE: MACBETH
John Wain

SHAKESPEARE: MEASURE FOR
MEASURE
G. K. Stead

SHAKESPEARE: THE MERCHANT
OF VENICE
John Wilders

SHAKESPEARE: A MIDSUMMER
NIGHT'S DREAM
A. W. Price

SHAKESPEARE: MUCH ADO
ABOUT NOTHING AND AS YOU
LIKE IT
John Russell Brown

SHAKESPEARE: OTHELLO
John Wain

SHAKESPEARE: RICHARD II
N. Brooke

SHAKESPEARE: THE SONNETS
Peter Jones

SHAKESPEARE: THE TEMPEST
D. J. Palmer

SHAKESPEARE: TROILUS AND
CRESSIDA
Priscilla Martin

SHAKESPEARE: TWELFTH NIGHT
D. J. Palmer

SHAKESPEARE: THE WINTER'S
TALE
Kenneth Muir

MACMILLAN STUDENTS' NOVELS

General Editor: JAMES GIBSON

The Macmillan Students' Novels are low-priced, new editions of major classics, aimed at the first examination candidate. Each volume contains:

* enough explanation and background material to make the novels accessible — and rewarding — to pupils with little or no previous knowledge of the author or the literary period;

* detailed notes elucidate matters of vocabulary, interpretation and historical background;

* eight pages of plates comprising facsimiles of manuscripts and early editions, portraits of the author and photographs of the geographical setting of the novels.

JANE AUSTEN: MANSFIELD PARK
Editor: Richard Wirdnam

JANE AUSTEN: NORTHANGER ABBEY
Editor: Raymond Wilson

JANE AUSTEN: PRIDE AND PREJUDICE
Editor: Raymond Wilson

JANE AUSTEN: SENSE AND SENSIBILITY
Editor: Raymond Wilson

JANE AUSTEN: PERSUASION
Editor: Richard Wirdnam

CHARLOTTE BRONTË: JANE EYRE
Editor: F. B. Pinion

EMILY BRONTË: WUTHERING HEIGHTS
Editor: Graham Handley

JOSEPH CONRAD: LORD JIM
Editor: Peter Hollindale

CHARLES DICKENS: GREAT EXPECTATIONS
Editor: James Gibson

CHARLES DICKENS: HARD TIMES
Editor: James Gibson

CHARLES DICKENS: OLIVER TWIST
Editor: Guy Williams

CHARLES DICKENS: A TALE OF TWO CITIES
Editor: James Gibson

GEORGE ELIOT: SILAS MARNER
Editor: Norman Howlings

GEORGE ELIOT: THE MILL ON THE FLOSS
Editor: Graham Handley

D. H. LAWRENCE: SONS AND LOVERS
Editor: James Gibson

D. H. LAWRENCE: THE RAINBOW
Editor: James Gibson

MARK TWAIN: HUCKLEBERRY FINN
Editor: Christopher Parry

THE MACMILLAN SHAKESPEARE

General Editor: PETER HOLLINDALE
Advisory Editor: PHILIP BROCKBANK

The Macmillan Shakespeare features:
* clear and uncluttered texts with modernised punctuation and spelling wherever possible;
* full explanatory notes printed on the page facing the relevant text for ease of reference;
* stimulating introductions which concentrate on content, dramatic effect, character and imagery, rather than mere dates and sources.

Above all, The Macmillan Shakespeare treats each play as a work for the theatre which can also be enjoyed on the page.

CORIOLANUS
Editor: Tony Parr

THE WINTER'S TALE
Editor: Christopher Parry

MUCH ADO ABOUT NOTHING
Editor: Jan McKeith

RICHARD II
Editor: Richard Adams

RICHARD III
Editor: Richard Adams

HENRY IV, PART I
Editor: Peter Hollindale

HENRY IV, PART II
Editor: Tony Parr

HENRY V
Editor: Brian Phythian

AS YOU LIKE IT
Editor: Peter Hollindale

A MIDSUMMER NIGHT'S DREAM
Editor: Norman Sanders

THE MERCHANT OF VENICE
Editor: Christopher Parry

THE TAMING OF THE SHREW
Editor: Robin Hood

TWELFTH NIGHT
Editor: E. A. J. Honigmann

THE TEMPEST
Editor: A. C. Spearing

ROMEO AND JULIET
Editor: James Gibson

JULIUS CAESAR
Editor: D. R. Elloway

MACBETH
Editor: D. R. Elloway

HAMLET
Editor: Nigel Alexander

ANTONY AND CLEOPATRA
Editors: Jan McKeith and
Richard Adams

OTHELLO
Editors: Celia Hilton and R. T. Jones

KING LEAR
Editor: Philip Edwards

MACMILLAN SHAKESPEARE VIDEO WORKSHOPS

DAVID WHITWORTH

Three unique book and video packages, each examining a particular aspect of Shakespeare's work; tragedy, comedy and the Roman plays. Designed for all students of Shakespeare, each package assumes no previous knowledge of the plays and can serve as a useful introduction to Shakespeare for 'O' and 'A' level candidates as well as for students at colleges and institutes of further, higher and adult education.

The material is based on the New Shakespeare Company Workshops at the Roundhouse, adapted and extended for television. By combining the resources of television and a small theatre company, this exploration of Shakespeare's plays offers insights into varied interpretations, presentation, styles of acting as well as useful background information.

While being no substitute for seeing the whole plays in performance, it is envisaged that these video cassettes will impart something of the original excitement of the theatrical experience, and serve as a welcome complement to textual analysis leading to an enriched and broader view of the plays.

Each package consists of:

* the Macmillan Shakespeare editions of the plays concerned;

* a video cassette available in VHS or Beta;

* a leaflet of teacher's notes.

THE TORTURED MIND
looks at the four tragedies Hamlet, Othello, Macbeth and King Lear.

THE COMIC SPIRIT
examines the comedies Much Ado About Nothing, Twelfth Night, A Midsummer Night's Dream, and As You Like It.

THE ROMAN PLAYS
Features Julius Caesar, Antony and Cleopatra
and Coriolanus